T0338445

CONCEPTUAL INFORMATION RETRIEVAL
A Case Study in Adaptive Partial Parsing

THE KLUWER INTERNATIONAL SERIES IN ENGINEERING AND COMPUTER SCIENCE

NATURAL LANGUAGE PROCESSING AND MACHINE TRANSLATION

Consulting Editor

Jaime Carbonell

Other books in the series:

EFFICIENT PARSING FOR NATURAL LANGUAGE: A FAST ALGORITHM FOR PRACTICAL SYSTEMS, M. Tomita
ISBN 0-89838-202-5

A NATURAL LANGUAGE INTERFACE FOR COMPUTER AIDED DESIGN, T. Samad
ISBN 0-89838-222-X

INTEGRATED NATURAL LANGUAGE DIALOGUE: A COMPUTATIONAL MODEL, R.E. Frederking
ISBN 0-89838-255-6

NAIVE SEMANTICS FOR NATURAL LANGUAGE UNDERSTANDING, K. Dahlgren
ISBN 0-89838-287-4

UNDERSTANDING EDITORIAL TEXT: A Computer Model of Argument Comprehension, S.J. Alvarado
ISBN: 0-7923-9123-3

NATURAL LANGUAGE GENERATION IN ARTIFICIAL INTELLIGENCE AND COMPUTATIONAL LINGUISTICS
Paris/Swartout/Mann
ISBN: 0-7923-9098-9

CURRENT ISSUES IN PARSING TECHNOLOGY
M. Tomita
ISBN: 0-7923-9131-4

CONCEPTUAL INFORMATION RETRIEVAL
A Case Study in Adaptive Partial Parsing

by

Michael L. Mauldin
Carnegie Mellon University

with a foreword by
Jaime G. Carbonell

KLUWER ACADEMIC PUBLISHERS
Boston/Dordrecht/London

Distributors for North America:
Kluwer Academic Publishers
101 Philip Drive
Assinippi Park
Norwell, Massachusetts 02061 USA

Distributors for all other countries:
Kluwer Academic Publishers Group
Distribution Centre
Post Office Box 322
3300 AH Dordrecht, THE NETHERLANDS

Library of Congress Cataloging-in-Publication Data
Mauldin, Michael L., 1959-
    Conceptual information retrieval : a case study in adaptive
partial parsing / by Michael L. Mauldin.
    p. cm. -- (The Kluwer international series in engineering and
computer science ; internal. vol. # 152. Natural language processing
and machine translation)
    Includes bibliographical references and index.
    ISBN 0-7923-9214-0 (alk. paper)
    1. Natural language processing (Computer science) 2. FERRET
(Information retrieval system) 3. Computational linguistics.
I. Title. II. Series : Kluwer international series in engineering
and computer science ; SECS 152. III. Series : Kluwer international
series in engineering and computer science. Natural language
processing and machine translation.
QA76.9.N38M38   1991
006.3'5--dc20   91-27108
                                  CIP

Printed on acid-free paper.

Printed in the United States of America

To my wife Michelle

TABLE OF CONTENTS

LIST OF FIGURES

FOREWORD

The information revolution is upon us. Whereas the industrial revolution heralded the systematic augmentation of human physical limitations by harnessing external energy sources, the information revolution strives to augment human memory and mental processing limitations by harnessing external computational resources. Computers can accumulate, transmit and output much more information and in a more timely fashion than more conventional printed or spoken media. Of greater interest, however, is the computer's ability to *process*, *classify* and *retrieve* information selectively in response to the needs of each human user. One cannot drink from the fire hydrant of information without being immediately flooded with irrelevant text. Recent technological advances such as optical character readers only exacerbate the problem by increasing the volume of electronic text. Just as steam and internal combustion engines brought powerful energy sources under control to yield useful work in the industrial revolution, so must we build computational engines that control and apply the vast information sources that they may yield useful knowledge.

Information science is the study of systematic means to control, classify, process and retrieve vast amounts of information in electronic form. In particular, several methodologies have been developed to classify texts manually by armies of human indexers, as illustrated quite clearly at the National Library of Medicine, and many computational techniques have been developed to search textual data bases automatically, such as full-text keyword searches. In general, the automated techniques are not quite as thorough or accurate as the manual ones, although they are far more economical and consistent. Keyword searches, in particular, suffer from the so-called *keyword barrier*: their inability to improve retrieval accuracy beyond a certain performance threshold. Consider for instance, searching for articles on Iraqi aggression towards its neighbors and therefore seeking text with the conjunction of words "Iraq," "Invasion," (OR "Kuwait," "Iran," "Saudi Arabia," ...). Texts on the US Invasion of southern Iraq from Saudi Arabia, and texts on Iraq's defense against Iran's counter invasion will be allowed through the filter. Worse yet, texts on "Saddam Hussein's military annexation of his small southern neighbor" may not pass the filter as not all the necessary keywords may be present. The filter, of course, can be improved, but only to a certain level — to the keyword barrier — if one must trade off precision and recall.

In order to progress beyond the keyword barrier, new methods are required, and many fields offer promising leads including: statistics, artificial intelligence (AI) and new advances in information science itself. Within AI, the field of natural language processing addresses issues of analyzing texts into syntactic and semantic representations. This form of text "understanding" provides hope that the computer may be able to see through paraphrases of the same concepts and thus retrieve texts such as the Saddam example above. Also semantic representations of text will block spurious retrievals based on unfortunate juxtaposition of keywords if the way in which they fit together implies a different set of concepts. In essence, we want to have retrieval by *key concept* rather than key word.

The AI approach, however, is far from a mature technology. General understanding of arbitrary text is arbitrarily difficult. A more promising approach in the near-term future is partial understanding of text leading to the extraction of key concepts without forming any complete understanding of the entire text or large portions thereof. This technology called *text skimming* offers hope in taming the information jungle in a more organized way than slash and burn keyword techniques, although requiring greater computational resources to accommodate its deeper processing. The FERRET system developed by Michael Mauldin and reported in this book develops precisely such an approach. Simpler versions of the same technological principles have already proven themselves in commercial applications, such as the TCS software developed at Carnegie Group Inc. Mauldin's methods incorporate full dictionary access (Webster's seventh), and automated adaptation to improve performance from user feedback using genetic algorithms.

These first cracks in the dreaded keyword barrier suggest that information revolution has yet quite a way to go as we improve the method for automated processing, classification and retrieval of electronic texts. This book tells the tale of one attempt to break the keyword barrier that has met with initial proven success, but there will be other attempts, some building on Mauldin's work and others with different technologies. There is an indisputable necessity to process accurately the ever-increasing volumes of textual information available in electronic form.

—Jaime Carbonell

PREFACE

Most information retrieval systems today use only the presence or absence of keywords to classify and retrieve texts. But simple word searches and frequency distributions do not capture the meaning behind the words, limiting the computer's ability to distinguish between relevant and irrelevant texts. We call this limit the *keyword barrier*.

We believe that breaking through the keyword barrier will require computer systems to *understand* the texts they process. This book describes FERRET: a full text, conceptual information retrieval system that uses a partial understanding of its texts to provide greater precision and recall performance than keyword search techniques. FERRET uses adaptive partial parsing to convert input texts into canonical case frames (called abstracts). User queries are similarly converted to case frames, and are matched to the abstracts using a case frame matcher.

FERRET's parser is derived from DeJong's FRUMP text skimming parser, with two important additions. First, FERRET is able to access an on-line English dictionary (*Webster's Seventh*) to handle unknown words, using script-based expectations to resolve multiple-meaning ambiguities. Second, a script learning component based on Holland's *genetic algorithms* takes user feedback on retrieval precision and augments FERRET's script repertoire, adapting the parser by filling holes in its episodic world knowledge.

Chapter 6 describes comparison studies of FERRET's retrieval performance on 1065 astronomy texts. These studies showed significant improvement in both *recall* and *precision* versus the standard boolean keyword search. Precision increased from 35 to 48 percent, and recall more than doubled, from 19 to 52 percent. The script learning component generated new scripts that significantly improved the recall performance of the basic FERRET system without significant effects on precision.

The robust parsing abilities demonstrated, with the depth and flexibility provided by on-line dictionary access and script learning, make partial parsing a useful foundation for many applications. The partial understanding provided by a canonical case frame representation is useful for tasks as diverse as information filtering, routing, categorization and summarization.

This book describes preliminary work in applying artificial intelligence and natural language processing to the problem of information retrieval: we are not telling you to throw away your current word-based retrieval system (yet). We are telling you how current work in these fields can be used to to build better retrieval systems in the future: systems that go beyond the keyword barrier because they understand what they read.

ACKNOWLEDGMENTS

FERRET began life as my dissertation project, and I owe much of its success to my advisor, Jaime Carbonell. When I had minor problems, his helpful direction and suggestions put me back on track. And when I was really stuck, unable to make any kind of progress, he would schedule a talk or a seminar for me, knowing full well that my fear of appearing in public unprepared was just the right impetus to get me going again. Thanks, Jaime.

I would also like to thank Jerry DeJong, on whose giant shoulders I have parsed farther than I could ever have hoped. His original work on FRUMP inspired me to write FERRET, and he generously provided his original data files and source code to get me started, as well as serving on my thesis committee to be sure that I used them correctly. This project literally could not have been accomplished without him.

Phil Hayes and Dana Scott rounded out my thesis committee. They kept me from hiding too well within the ivory tower of CMU and pressured me to make my work relevant and understandable beyond the concrete walls of Wean Hall.

Thanks also to the G. & C. Merriam Company, for use of the on-line *Webster's Seventh Dictionary*, to the folks at STARDATE and the University of Texas McDonald Observatory, for the use of STARDATE radio scripts for the astronomy database, and to Dow Jones and Company, for access to the Dow Jones newswire service, in addition to their generous funding. Without these resources, FERRET would be an "interesting" but minor curiosity.

Many people have helped me by kibitzing, arguing, and discussing various aspects on this work. Many thanks to Hans Berliner, Mark Boggs, David Evans, Robert Frederking, Gordon Goetsch, John Holland, Karen Kukich, David Lewis, Ira Monarch, Steve Morrison, Stephen Smith, Karen Sparck Jones, and Rich Thomason. Thanks, too, to all of the students who took the time to respond to the user query survey.

Lastly I must give due credit to the Carnegie Mellon School of Computer Science, the Center for Machine Translation, my officemates past and present, and the INTERNET and USENET communities, for providing the nutrient rich medium in which this project germinated and grew to bear fruit.

Michael L. Mauldin

CONCEPTUAL INFORMATION RETRIEVAL
A Case Study in Adaptive Partial Parsing

Chapter 1
INTRODUCTION

I only ask for information.
—Miss Rosa Dartle
David Copperfield, Ch. 20

1.1. Motivation

The advent of electronic publishing has resulted in an avalanche of computer readable text. Newspapers, books, reports and articles are generated with help from computers, transmitted by computers, and stored in computers. Bibliographic databases list every book, article, and report published. Lawyers have databases listing doctor's malpractice cases, and doctors have databases listing litigious patients [Bradley 86], [Time 86]. Whole encyclopedias are now published on laser disks. At Carnegie Mellon, researchers are building an on-line library of artificial intelligence literature that already contains bibliographic references, and will soon contain the full texts of technical reports and conference papers [Arms & Holzhauser 88].

Until very recently, there have been only three major strategies for locating individual texts within such large collections of information. The oldest method is to ask a wise sage who had read every book and could tell which one contained the necessary information and where the book was located. When the number of books began to exceed the limits of human memory, categorizations were developed, such as the Dewey decimal system and more recently the Library of Congress subject headings. Each text is assigned a pigeonhole, and the work can only be found by knowing into which pigeonhole one must look. With the computer came the possibility of searching through the entire collection to find words and phrases that identify a text as containing the information being sought. This "free text searching" ability meant that the searcher did not have to rely on someone else assigning the book to a particular category, but the searcher did need to know which words to use when looking for the text.

The FERRET project was motivated by Blair and Maron's study of STAIRS, a major commercial information retrieval system, as used in a large law firm [Blair & Maron 85a], [Blair & Maron 85b], [Salton 86]. They found that on average, and unknown to the people using the system, STAIRS was retrieving only 1 in 5 documents relevant to the questions that were asked of it. Worse still, this was not the fault of the designers of STAIRS, one of the best examples of its kind. It was an inherent limitation of the ability of this approach to information retrieval.

Blair and Maron list many problems with textual databases, and most of their findings fall into two categories:

- Phraseology: synonyms, slang and jargon terms obscure the meaning of the text, making it very difficult to locate by keyword approaches.
- Granularity: as database size increases, increasingly fine-grained searches are necessary. Retrieval techniques that only consider the presence or absence of words cannot distinguish different relationships between the same words, and retrieve far more documents than the user considers relevant [Carbonell & Thomason 86].

Blair and Maron conclude that "there are theoretical reasons why full-text retrieval systems applied to large databases are unlikely to perform well." Their argument is a probabilistic one based on likelihood of occurrence of keywords. Their solution is to return to manual indexing of documents. Our answer is to give up on easily programmed operations such as word counting, bite the proverbial bullet, and build an information retrieval system that can at least partially *understand* the text. With even a partial understanding of a text, the computer should be better able to determine whether the text is relevant to the user's query.

1.2. The Keyword Barrier

The crucial problem of current information retrieval technology is that systems relying solely on the presence or absence of a word are inherently limited in their ability to distinguish relevant and irrelevant texts. Some research efforts have attempted to improve retrieval performance by indexing on phrases rather than on words [Fagan 87a], by adding synonym information, and by using frequency of words [Salton 86]. But the gains from these refinements have been disappointing. The limits of word-based retrieval systems have been previously explored in [Lesk 85] and [Metzler et al. 84].

The English language as used in real texts has many complicating, unsystematic features that confound and confuse simple, word-based information retrieval systems. The most difficult of these features are:

Synonymy   In the Blair and Maron example, various terms were used to describe the same objects: girder, I-beam, structural member. Although thesauri are a focus of current research in information retrieval, there are problems with ambiguity as well. Failure to deal with synonymy reduces recall performance, because texts that use synonymous terms do not match the user query, and are never retrieved.

Polysemy   Just as one meaning can be represented by multiple words, a single word can have multiple meanings. "Beam" is a type of board in carpentry, the width of a ship in nautical terminology, and a tightly focused electromagnetic emission in radio terminology. Polysemous words reduce precision, and attempts to improve precision by using phrases instead of ambiguous words can also reduce recall where the phrases can be constructed in multiple ways. Worse still, synonymy and polysemy can occur together; see Figure 1-1 for such an example.

	"stringer"	"ledger"	"post"	"copy"
Carpentry	stairway support	horizontal support	vertical support	
Accounting		book	to enter a transaction	
Computing			send a message	duplicate
Newpapers	employee		name of newspaper	text

Figure 1-1: Synonymy and Polysemy

Anaphora   Pronominal references such as "it" can hide sentences from queries that rely on full exposition. This may explain why word-based text searches on manually written abstracts have had better recall performance than searches done on the full text [Salton 86]. Use of anaphoric reference tends to disperse the words related to a concept throughout a text, and can prevent simple word-based or syntax-based retrieval methods from detecting a search term.*

Variability

Searches that rely on phrases may miss alternative sentence constructions; for example, a "dual port disk drive" is the same thing as a "disk drive with 2 ports."

Metaphor

Stocks "soar" and "plunge," new employees "sink or swim," and a *Time* article about selling used computers reads "Computer dinosaurs live again." Understanding these phrases has less to do with the words and more to do with the ideas behind them [Carbonell 82].

Relations

Some concepts simply do not have single word labels, and therefore are represented by phrases, the components of which may have other meanings. Differentiating these concepts may depend on the relationships between the sentence components, and not their presence or absence. Consider the following example of a crime database, from Carbonell. Any word-based searches for

juvenile victims of crime

would probably also retrieved the more numerous texts about

victims of juvenile crime

Another example, taken from the Astronomy database described in Section 6.1.3, exhibits a similar pair of words. The actual sentence is

You can probably spot Jupiter now.

but this would be easily confused by searches for

The Great Red Spot of Jupiter.

---

*Abstracts contain few anaphoric references, because they are meant to be self-contained, and are often written with keyword retrieval in mind.

Context sensitivity Some phrases have more than one possible interpretation and can only be understood in the context of the surrounding text. Double entendres and garden path sentences fall into this category. Here are some examples of sentences and phrases for which their are multiple interpretations:

Congressman launches NASA probe.

Your Culligan man can be found under water in the yellow pages.

Ladies' dresses half off.

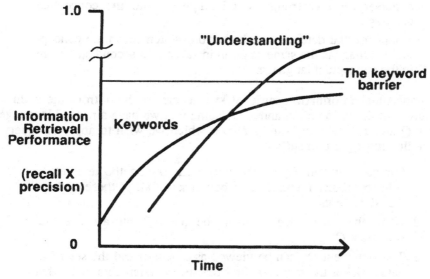

Figure 1-2: The Keyword Barrier

Word-based systems that cannot deal with synonymy, polysemy, metaphor, and the other complications of real language must have some upper bound on their retrieval performance. We have called this limit the "keyword barrier," and depict it graphically in Figure 1-2. Further efforts to enhance and refine the word-based approach to information retrieval may push the performance closer to the asymptote, but will give less and less payback. We propose that recent advances in artificial intelligence, such as knowledge representation, natural language parsing, and tree structure matching can be combined into a system that uses computer understanding of texts to push retrieval performance beyond the keyword barrier.

1.3. Beyond the Keyword Barrier: Conceptual Matching

The keyword barrier exists because there is no perfect correlation between matching words and matching meaning. As the examples in the previous section show, the correlation may be very low indeed. So the necessary solution to the problem of increasing retrieval performance is to give up on matching words and to match concepts instead. That requires three things:

- a conceptual language to represent meanings
- a parser for converting natural language into the conceptual language
- a matcher that determines whether one statement in the conceptual language is the same as or an instance of a second statement in the conceptual language.

A conceptual information retrieval system can be built from these three resources in the following manner. Assume that we have a natural language query Q and a collection of texts T over which we wish to apply the query. The following algorithm suffices:

1. For each text in T, run the parser to convert the text into a conceptual statement. Let T^c be the set of all of these conceptual statements.

2. Using the same parser, convert the query Q into a conceptual statement Q^c.

3. The statement Q^c can be viewed as a pattern and the set T^c as data. Using the matcher, find the set of statements in T^c that are the same as or instances of the query statement Q^c. Call this set T_r^c.

4. Now find the set of texts in the original T that correspond to the matched statements in T_r^c. Call this set T_r.

The set T_r is the set of retrieved documents for the query Q from the database T. If the parser accurately converts text to concepts and the conceptual matcher accurately relates like concepts, then the parsing and matching operations should form a homomorphism with human relevance judgements (that is, the retrieved documents should be all and only those texts relevant to the original query). Section 4.1.1 describes this "relevance homomorphism assumption" in more detail.

So far we have made no requirements of the conceptual language assumed above. But for the matching process above to be feasible, the underlying conceptual language must be *canonical*. That means that all English constructions that have the same basic meaning must be parsed into the same representation. In this way, the matcher must only determine whether the conceptual statements are structurally the same, and canonicality will assure that the surface sentences are related.

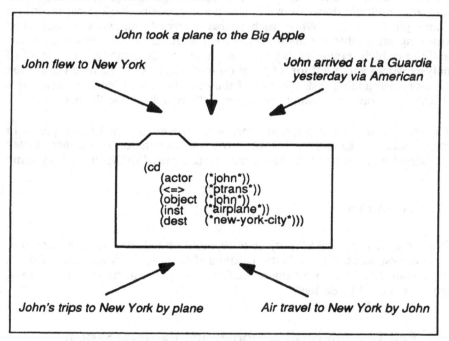

Figure 1-3: Canonicality of CD representation improves recall

One such canonical knowledge representation language is "Conceptual Dependency Theory, " sometimes shortened to "CD Theory" [Schank et al. 75], [Schank & Riesbeck 81]. Figure 1-3 shows graphically how different sentences with the same basic meaning are given the same representation as a conceptual dependency graph. Note that for the matcher to determine that the sentence *"John arrived at La Guardia"* matches the query *"Air travel to New York by John"*, the matcher must be able to determine that La Guardia is in New York. So the matcher must have access to world knowledge as well as the output from the parser.

How then is the raw English text, with its ambiguity, context sensitivity, and other difficult linguistic features, converted into a neat, canonical representation? Full natural language parsers have been built to do this job (for example, see [Schank & Riesbeck 81], [Sparck Jones & Wilks 83], [Carbonell & Thomason 86] and [Tomita 86]), but they tend to be limited in their ability to handle multiple domains, and are often slow and "brittle"—unable to handle texts with grammatical errors or unusual sentence constructions. An alternative to full parsing is "text skimming." One example is the FRUMP parser [DeJong, G. 79a], which can extract the general meaning of a text, ignoring or suppressing the details, and cope with texts from multiple domains, recognizing and choosing the correct meanings of ambiguous words. While such coarse levels of analysis can make text skimming unsuitable for applications such as machine translation or query handling (which require highly accurate retention of meaning), this level of analysis works very well for information retrieval tasks. Machine translation is a more demanding task because of the need to convey nuance, whereas a retrieval need only ascertain the concept well enough to find the document.

Chapter 3 discusses conceptual dependency theory and the FRUMP parser in more detail, and Chapter 4 describes the implementation of the MCFRUMP text skimming parser and the case frame matcher used in the FERRET system.

1.4. Definitions

The goal of the FERRET project is to build and demonstrate a computer retrieval system capable of better distinguishing a few relevant texts from a larger number of irrelevant ones. Before this goal can be stated precisely, some terms must be defined.

1.4.1. Full Text Information Storage and Retrieval System

Many information retrieval systems are *bibliographic*. They contain short descriptions of documents, rather than the full text of the documents themselves. With ever increasing memory capacity, it seems likely that the full text of most documents will be available on-line in the not too distant future. Furthermore, most texts do not come with high quality, detailed abstracts, or even lists of standard, approved keywords. To study retrieval of abstracts is to beg the question of where the abstracts come from. For these two reasons, this project comprises only the study of full-text retrieval systems.

1.4.2. Boolean Keyword Query System

In Chapter 6, we will compare FERRET's performance to a typical "boolean keyword query system." Throughout this book, the terms "keyword system," "keyword search," and "word-based" retrieval system will be synonymous with boolean keyword query. We take the following operations as necessary and sufficient to be in this class:

- find the set of documents containing a particular word
- find the set of documents containing a particular word stem
- boolean combinations of sets using intersection, union, and complement (usually called AND, OR, and NOT)
- (optional) the adjacency operator, extracts sets of documents containing one word within a given distance from a second word (sometimes called ADJ or NEARX).

The STAIRS system studied by Blair and Maron implements all of these operations (plus others), and is therefore classified as a boolean keyword query system.

1.4.3. Conceptual Dependency, Case Frames

The case frames used are based on Conceptual Dependency theory as described in [Schank et al. 75], [Schank & Riesbeck 81]. The slots used follow the general scheme laid out by Schank, but we have not strictly adhered to his list of primitive actions. The frames are implemented using the FRAMEKIT package built at Carnegie Mellon [Carbonell & Joseph 85], [Nyberg 88]. FRAMEKIT implements a frame-based knowledge representation providing frames, inheritance (including tangled hierarchies), demons (such as IF-NEEDED and IF-ADDED), and multiple views. The inheritance system allows information common to a class of words to be stored efficiently.

1.4.4. Texts

The terms "document," "message," "narrative," "post" "script," "story," "text" and "wire" can all refer to the input texts that are stored in a retrieval system. The most confusing is "script," which is used by the people at the University of Texas to describe the STARDATE texts. These texts are really scripts for a daily radio program put out by the McDonald Observatory. We will endeavor throughout to use "script" solely to refer to sketchy scripts (units of episodic knowledge), but be aware that other references to STARDATE might mention "STARDATE scripts."

1.4.5. Scripts

Case frame patterns are used to represent knowledge of common events and sequences of events. We use the term "script" to describe such a case frame pattern. These patterns correspond most closely the the term "sketchy script" used by DeJong in his FRUMP system, but for the most part FERRET scripts are even smaller. Since "Even Sketchier Scripts" is too wordy, We will refer to them as merely "scripts."

1.4.6. Abstracts

An abstract is a summary of something larger. In FERRET, when a text has been parsed, the result is an *instantiated sketchy script pattern*, that is a pattern where the variables have been bound to specific fillers. We call these instantiated sketchy scripts "abstracts," since they are used in FERRET in exactly the same way abstracts are used in bibliographic databases to describe other texts. For some domains, the input texts might indeed be abstracts of still larger texts, but that will not be true of the domains discussed in this book.

1.4.7. Understanding

Throughout this book, we will often use the word "understand," as in "The parser correctly understood 60 percent of the texts," or "The MCFRUMP parser does not understand 'atmosphere' in this context." By "understand," we mean that the parser generates an instantiated sketchy script (or abstract, as defined above) that correctly portrays the meaning of the original sentence at a coarse level of detail. Thus in some sentences, nuances may be lost during the parsing, but the general meaning is conveyed, and the sentence will have been said to be "correctly understood."

It is not within the scope of this book to defend the epistemological and ontological correctness of describing computers as capable of understanding in the human sense. This anthropomorphic metaphor is used merely for the sake of brevity.

1.5. Performance Measures for Information Retrieval

1.5.1. Precision

Precision is a standard measure of how effectively an information retrieval system operates. It is the ratio of documents retrieved by the system that are actually relevant to the query given by the user divided by the total number of documents retrieved. Precision is usually expressed as a percentage. High precision means that few irrelevant documents are retrieved. Low precision means many irrelevant documents are retrieved. Most modern information retrieval system are capable of demonstrating high precision for moderately sized databases.

1.5.2. Recall

Recall is another standard measure of the effectiveness of an information retrieval system. There may be many documents in the database that the user would consider relevant, but only some will be retrieved by the system. The ratio of the total number of relevant texts retrieved by the system number by the total number of relevant texts in the database is the recall performance, also expressed as a percentage. In reality the recall performance is difficult to measure. It requires an omniscient determination of the set of relevant documents. In practice it is possible to place an upper bound on the recall performance of a system by finding documents that should have been retrieved but were not. This bound may be improved by spending more and more time manually searching for relevant documents that were missed by the retrieval system. In contrast to the high precision performance typical of modern retrieval systems, Blair and Maron report that STAIRS found only a fifth of the documents the user would consider relevant. That one fifth is an upper bound — the real number might even be smaller.

1.5.3. Response Time

Response time is the elapsed time between the submission of a query by the user and the presentation to the user of the texts retrieved by that query. Boolean keyword query systems based on inverted files usually have very good response times; usually no more than a few seconds. FERRET as currently implemented is very slow. Sections 4.5 and 7.3.2 give suggestions for providing fast response time with a FERRET-like retrieval system.

1.5.4. Maintenance

Maintenance refers to all human labor required to keep the system working. This includes the human effort needed to add texts to the database; for some systems this may be a non-trivial amount of work. For example, some systems require the user to assign index terms to a text — for such a database to display both high precision and high recall may entail an enormous amount of work for the human indexer. Since FERRET classifies input texts automatically, it has the *potential* to significantly reduce the effort required for database maintenance.

This refers to the amount of hand-coding *per input document*, which is small, compared to the amount of hand-coding required to maintain FERRET's knowledge base, which is large. The hope is that the knowledge base need only be built once (or once per domain).

1.6. Goals of the FERRET project

The central goal of this project is to build and demonstrate a *full text information storage and retrieval system* called FERRET that used *case frames* to provide a conceptual representation of texts and to show that this retrieval system provides better recall and precision performance than is possible with a boolean keyword retrieval system. The algorithms used to implement this system should not require unreasonable amount of *maintenance*, and must be capable of providing fast *response time*.

This major goal can be subdivided into the following four distinct objectives:

1.6.1. Objective 1: Demonstrate conceptual matching on real texts

The most basic objective of this project is to demonstrate a complete information storage and retrieval system working on real texts that uses conceptual matching as the basis of its retrieval mechanism. The FERRET system,
based on the conceptual understanding ability of the MCFRUMP parser, is
described and examples are shown in Chapter 4. The effectiveness of the
conceptual matching is described in Chapter 6, especially Section 6.4.

One of the goals in the succinct statement above is that the system must be
capable of fast response time; Sections 4.5 and 7.3.2 show how the data
structures and representations used in FERRET can be searched within a
constant factor of the speed achieved by keyword systems based on inverted
files.

1.6.2. Objective 2: Use an on-line dictionary to augment lexical knowledge

Knowledge-based systems can require large amounts of domain and world
knowledge. To improve the parser's coverage without undue human effort in
building massive lexicons, the FERRET system is able to tap information
already available in computer form, specifically the *Webster's Seventh
Dictionary*.

The dictionary access component is discussed in Section 4.4. The effectiveness of the dictionary component is discussed in Section 6.3.

1.6.3. Objective 3: Use Genetic learning to augment script knowledge

The goal of low maintenance also implies that, where possible, the system
must be able to learn concepts within its domain with minimal human effort
involved. It should not be necessary for the knowledge base implementors to
forsee every possible concept that the retrieval system will ever have to
match.

The learning component is described in Chapter 5, and its effectiveness is
described in Section 6.4.5. The learning component generated modifications
of scripts that significantly improved FERRET's recall performance at the
expense of a slight drop in precision.

1.6.4. Objective 4: Provide better recall and precision than keyword systems

The ultimate objective of this work is to demonstrate that conceptual understanding provides better retrieval performance; ideally resulting in a substantial increase in both recall and precision performance.

Section 6.4 compares the recall and precision performance of the FERRET system with a typical boolean keyword query system on a sample of 44 user queries over a database of 1035 texts, and describes the methodology of the experiments. FERRET is shown to have significantly greater precision, and to have retrieved more than twice as many relevant documents as the simple boolean keyword search.

1.7. Learning

The attempt to add machine learning to the parser is a response to the requirement that maintaining the retrieval system must not require unreasonable human effort. Parsers require such a wealth of knowledge to understand large amounts of real text that is may be too expensive to build the entire knowledge base by hand. If the computer can learn some or all of what it needs to parse new texts coming into the system, then the goal of low maintenance may be met.

Section 2.5 discusses some current applications of machine learning to natural language processing. Chapter 5 describes the implementation of genetic learning used in FERRET, and Section 6.4.5 describes the effectiveness of the learning and gives samples of newly learned scripts.

1.8. Chapter Overview

This book describes a new approach to information retrieval, conceptual understanding and matching of texts to queries, and describes one study of its effectiveness versus the standard boolean keyword retrieval for a collection of texts about astronomy. Portions of the results presented here have appeared in [Mauldin 86a] and [Mauldin et al. 87].

The chapters are organized as follows:

Chapter 1, this chapter, introduces the problem of low recall performance in current information retrieval systems. We define the standard measures of precision and recall, as well as other terms that will be used throughout this book. The keyword barrier is defined and discussed, and conceptual matching is proposed as a solution to this barrier. Machine learning is introduced as a necessary step for reducing the human effort involved in classifying very large amounts of machine readable text.

Chapter 2, **Current Approaches**, describes the state of the art in information retrieval, including standard boolean keyword search and more recent work in frequency based techniques, and in semantic retrieval. The inherent problems with word-based and syntax-based retrieval systems are discussed, and machine learning approaches to natural language processing are also described.

Chapter 3, **Conceptual Understanding**, discusses knowledge representation techniques including syntactic methods, semantic grammars, and case frame methods. The FRUMP parser is described in detail, and its advantages and limitations for information retrieval are discussed as well.

Chapter 4, **Ferret**, describes the architecture and components of the FERRET retrieval system, including its parser, dictionary interface, and retrieval system based on case frame matching. A detailed, annotated transcript of parsing and retrieval is given.

Chapter 5, **Learning**, describes both the basic genetic algorithm and the modifications made for FERRET to provide a learning component that hypothesizes and evaluates new scripts so that the system can understand and retrieve more texts than can be found with the basic FERRET system. Examples of newly learned scripts are also given.

Chapter 6, **Empirical Studies**, describes several experiments analyzing the parser, the effectiveness of the dictionary interface, and most importantly a comparison of the retrieval performance (both precision and recall) of the FERRET system (with and without learning) versus the standard boolean keyword retrieval technique. When compared to keyword-based retrieval performance, the FERRET system is shown to increase precision from

35 percent to 50 percent, and to have 50 percent greater recall without learning and 100 percent greater recall with script learning.

Chapter 7, **Conclusion and Future Work**, describes the contributions made by the FERRET project, including a demonstration of a working knowledge-based information retrieval system that uses an on-line dictionary and an automatic script learning component to index and retrieve texts with significant comparative improvement over the recall and precision performance of keyword system performance on the same domain. Chapter 7 also describes the work necessary to convert this research result into a practical commercial retrieval system, and the applications of the techniques of text skimming, conceptual matching, dictionary access, and machine learning to various text processing, storage and retrieval tasks.

Appendix A, **Sample Data Structures**, gives examples of all of the major data structures and knowledge sources used by the FERRET system.

Appendix B, **User Queries**, gives the user queries that were the basis of the empirical study in Chapter 6, and a sample survey form showing how the user queries were collected.

Appendix C, **Raw Data**, gives the parsing and retrieval performance of FERRET and keyword search for each of the queries described in Appendix B.

Appendix D, **Number and Date grammars**, gives the LEX grammars used by the text scanner to preprocess the incoming text, to extract dates, numbers, and other lexical tokens, and to convert the stream of characters into tokens suitable for Lisp based processing.

Chapter 2
CURRENT APPROACHES

Information Retrieval, eh? The Big Boys!
—Terry Gilliam
Brazil

An information retrieval system takes a user query and a database of texts and classifies the texts according to how relevant they are to the query. Information retrieval techniques can themselves be classified according to several dimensions. One of the most useful distinctions depends on when a text is processed: during initial entry, or during retrieval request (query).

Some systems store texts unprocessed and do all of their computation after the query is given. Others assign each text to one or more predetermined categories when the document is entered into the database, thus doing the bulk of their computation ahead of time. Some schemes do significant processing both when texts are entered and when they are retrieved.

This continuum between pre-processing and post-processing is very similar to a division used by the information retrieval community: into *precoordinate* and *postcoordinate*. According to Salton [Salton & McGill 83], the terms have very specific meanings. Each document is represented by a collection of index terms. In postcoordinate systems, the terms are combined at search time, in precoordinate systems, the terms are related when the document is indexed, and the index may then be a compound reflecting the relationship between the terms.

Without taking too much liberty, we relax these definitions as follows:

Precoordinate   describes those systems that do the bulk of the classification before any queries are given. Such systems typically assign each document to one or more of a prespecified set of classes at index time.

Postcoordinate   describes those systems that do the bulk of their clas-
                      sification after the query is given, based on the the infor-
                      mation requested in the query.

2.1. Postcoordinate Systems

These are systems that do the lion's share of their work after a query is
given. Often they must separately process each text in the database, making
a series of decisions about each text's relevance to the query at hand. Some
systems, such as *inverted file methods*, pre-compute a data structure that
allows them to reduce a linear search process to a much faster pre-indexed
search.

2.1.1. Free Text String Searching

The simplest retrieval systems match texts by searching for occurrences of
a *search string* anywhere in the document. String searching is incorporated
into a variety of computer systems for dealing with collections of text.
Computer mail systems and text editors often have string searching
commands built in. Examples here at Carnegie Mellon include the EMACS
text editor [Gosling 83], the USENET news reading program [Horton 83].

Regular expressions provide the basis for a more sophisticated string
matching algorithm, and this technique is used by perhaps the most widely
used retrieval system in university computing: the Unix GREP command [Bell
Labs 79]. The word ''grep'' stands for ''global regular expression pattern.''
Indeed, the staff at McDonald Observatory were unimpressed by our efforts
to index their library of old radio scripts with FERRET. They use GREP to find
old stories on a particular topic. It is simple and effective for them; because
they know precisely what words to look for, they just need only to search for
files containing those words.

One problem with string search retrieval is that all of the computation
comes after the user has entered the query, for moderate or large amounts of
text the response times can be exceedingly slow. One solution is to use
special hardware. Digital Equipment's VAX computer has a special machine
instruction to search a block of memory for a given string. Roger Haskin at
the University of Illinois designed and built special hardware for implementing fast string searches of large text databases using non-deterministic finite

state automata, which are very similar to the GREP command [Haskin 80]. These are but two examples of using hardware to speed up string searching.

2.1.2. Inverted File Methods

By far the most successful and prevalent information retrieval systems today are based on inverted files. The best single discussion of this technique is Salton's *Modern Information Retrieval* [Salton & McGill 83]. See also [Teskey 82].

The basic idea is to trade storage space for retrieval time. The database is viewed as a collection of files. An alphabetized list of words is created. For each occurrence of a word in a file, an entry is created on the list for that word with a pointer back to the file. In some systems, the pointer indicates the position in the file where the word occurs, while in other systems the pointer merely indicates that the word appears in the file one or more times. Common words such as "the" and "of" are excluded from the indexing (the list of words not to index is called a "stop list"). Figure 2-1 shows a small example of an inverted file.

At retrieval time, the words in the query are looked up in the inverted file. Then the lists of documents containing the words are intersected (or unioned) to produce the list of texts matching the query. Since the list lookup can be done in constant time using hash tables, or logarithmic time using sorted lists or trees, the time required to process a query is dependent mainly on the number of documents containing each search term. This is usually much smaller than the total database. Fast retrieval time is the main advantage of these inverted files.

Some systems (such as STAIRS [Salton 86]) add the notion of proximity, usually implemented as an *adjacency* operator, or a *within* operator. For systems that store the position of each occurrence of the index terms, the adjacency operator can be implemented by checking that the position of the second term is exactly one more than the position of the first term. For the example in Figure 2-1, the query:

```
[ brown ADJ fox ]
```

gives us the following occurrence lists:

```
brown           (1  3)   (2  2)
fox             (1  4)   (2  4)
```

File 1		Inverted Index, (file# position)	
The quick brown fox jumped		brown	(1 3) (2 2)
over the lazy dog.		code	(3 15)
		dog	(1 9) (2 7)
		evaluation	(3 2)
File2		fox	(1 4) (2 4)
		improve	(3 4)
My brown Volkswagen Fox		jumped	(1 5)
is no dog when it comes		jumps	(3 12)
to performance.		lazy	(1 8) (3 1)
		performance	(2 12) (3 6)
File 3		quick	(1 2)
		reduce	(3 8)
Lazy evaluation can improve		volkswagen	(2 3)
system performance, and			
reduce the number of jumps			
in your code.			

Figure 2-1: An Example of Inverted Files

For file number one, we have positions 3 and 4, so file one passes the adjacency test, but the second file fails since the words are at positions 2 and 4. The same idea can be used to implement a WITHIN operator that is true only if the first and second terms are within some specified numbers of words of each other.

Another common extension is word stemming. For example, STAIRS uses the "$" operator to indicate that any word with a given prefix should be matched. For our little example, the query:

    [jump$]

gives occurrence lists:

    jumped   (1 5)
    jumps   (3 12)

Where the inverted file is kept in alphabetical order, the terms matching a given prefix are all together, making this operator simple to implement.

Most inverted file systems use "boolean keyword queries" in their retrieval processing. That means that the set of texts matching each term in the query are combined using the set operations of intersection, union, and complementation to produce a final set of retrieved documents.

For example, using our three test files from Figure 2-1, the query:

```
[ jump$ OR perform$ AND (NOT code) ]
```

would retrieve files 1 and 2, but not 3. The use of the NOT operator is considered very dangerous, because a perfectly relevant text might contain the negated word or phrase in some unimportant or unrelated clause, causing the document to be missed.

2.1.3. Sampling of Inverted File Systems

These systems all use inverted files to provide swift response times. This list is not exhaustive; it is only a sampling of the major commercial systems.

Dialog   Lockheed Information Systems commercial database system. Provides boolean retrieval based on inverted keywords, allows truncated search terms and word order adjacency testing [Salton & McGill 83].

Stairs   IBM's commercial information retrieval system. Also provides boolean retrieval based on inverted keywords, truncated search terms and word order adjacency testing [Blair & Maron 85a], [Salton & McGill 83].

Orbit, Medlars   The National Library of Medicine's attempt to automate the Index Medicus. Provides simple boolean keyword queries and string searches [Salton & McGill 83].

LEXIS   Mead Data Central's legal database service. LEXIS provides boolean queries of keywords, but also include simple morphology information [Salton & McGill 83].

Status   Computer Science and Systems Division A.E.R.E., boolean query, field search, and truncation, plus report generation, macros facilities and thesaurus information [Teskey 82].

2.1.4. Similarity Measures, Clustering

The SMART information retrieval system from Cornell [Salton 73], [Salton & Lesk 68], [Salton & McGill 83] uses a similarity measure based on word frequency to determine whether a document is similar to other documents known to be relevant to the user's query. To find the degree of similarity between two documents, the method is to:

- determine frequencies of each index term in the document collection.
- for any two documents, view the frequency lists for those documents as vectors in multidimensional space, and calculate the cosine of the angle between the two vectors.

The problem with this approach is that a typical user query will not have enough words to give a statistically meaningful frequency vector: this method only works for measuring the differences between two documents.

SMART incorporates some suffix removal rules to calculate frequencies based on the stem rather than the whole word.

Word frequency systems have been proposed as alternatives to boolean keyword search, and in some cases have demonstrated improved recall and precision performance. Nonetheless, they seem not to have made much impact on commercial information retrieval. Some early work on the subject was done at Ohio state by James Cameron [Cameron 72]. Clement Yu provided a thorough discussion of the use of frequency methods to "pseudoclassify" documents [Yu 73].

2.1.5. Higher Order Statistics: Latent Semantic Indexing

The most impressive use of word frequencies is "Latent Semantic Indexing." [Deerwester et al. 90], [Dumais et al. 88], [Furnas et al. 88], [Landauer & Littman 90]. By taking advantage of the "implicit higher-order structure in the association of terms with documents," this technique provides a metric that can be used to measure the "closeness" of words with documents, words with words, or documents with documents.

By the use of singular-value decomposition, a larger matrix of term/document associations is decomposed into three singular matrices.

Then a reduced set of matrices is chosen by retaining only the 100 or so largest singular values. The reduced matrix is the closest approximation of the original term/document matrix in a least-squares sense [Deerwester et al. 90]. Each term or document is represented as a vector in this 100 dimensional space, and the distance between any two words or documents is determined by taking the cosine of the angle between their two vectors.

Initial experiments using LSI on standard IR test collections is "encouraging," with retrieval performance comparable to the SMART system on one collection and superior in another [Deerwester et al. 90].

The LSI technique solves the synonymy problem very effectively, in that terms with similar meanings often end up very close to each other in the reduced dimensional space. This allows queries using one term to retrieve documents by similarity to a synonym,

Polysemy remains a problem, however, because the indexing is done by words and not by word senses. As a result a word is represented by the vector sum of its various meanings. In spaces where these vectors point in very different directions, the vector sum may not be close to any of the real meanings of the word.

Another potential problem is scale: the decomposition process requires $O(N^3)$ cpu time for N input documents. While document collections of 10,000 are feasible on today's computers, collections of millions of documents may not be amenable to this kind of analysis.

2.1.6. Adaptive Methods

Another word-based technique is "relevance feedback." After an initial query the user selects the relevant articles from the retrieved set and similarity measures are recalculated. The revised measures are used to query the database again, resulting in a new set of documents, and the process continues until the search converges or the user is satisfied with the documents retrieved up to that point.

David Waltz of Thinking Machines, Inc. described his company's implementation of the technique at the 1987 Conference of The National Federation of Abstracting and Information Services in Washington, DC. He claimed that the system gives both high recall performance and high precision (over 80 percent). Because it runs on the high-powered Connection Machine, each iteration requires less than a second [Waltz 87].

Salton describes the use of relevance feedback as implemented in the SMART system, and claims precision improvements between 20 and 50 percent depending on the recall performance [Salton & McGill 83]. Recall that each document is represented by a frequency vector; SMART depends on the assumption that similar documents are clustered together in this space. Each document or query is simply a point in this high-dimensional space. So a set of documents has an "average" that is just the centroid of these points representing each document. If the user's relevance judgments of a set of retrieval documents are known, then the sets of all relevant and irrelevant documents is approximated by the sets of relevant and irrelevant retrieved texts. Given one pair of sets, a new query can be generated by subtracting the irrelevant documents D_{N-R} from the relevant set D_R as follows:

$$(Q_{opt})_k = C \left(\sum_{i \in D_R} TERM_{ik} - \sum_{i \in D_{N-R}} TERM_{ik} \right)]$$

Where the documents are really clustered, one or two iterations of this process suffice to increase retrieval performance, and further iterations are less helpful.

Relevance feedback is a technique that can be applied to any retrieval system capable of ranking documents in order of their estimated relevance to the query, and often results in improved precision [Dumais 90]. Thus it may be viewed not as a retrieval technique in its own right, but more as a performance enhancement to several types of retrieval systems.

Another approach to adaptive retrieval based on parallel computation is the AIR system built by Rik Belew at the University of Michigan [Belew 87a]. AIR uses an associative network to store connections between documents where links include author's name and other index terms. Using user feedback about the relevance of retrieved texts, the system modifies weights on the links in the network and creates new links to attempt to learn the semantics of its domain.

2.2. Precoordinate Systems

In precoordinate systems, documents are assigned to one or more predetermined categories (like "pigeon-holes"). On retrieval, the user enters the name of a category or "index term" and all documents assigned to that category are retrieved. Almost all manual Library card catalogs are based on such a system where the pigeon-holes are called "subject headings." In such manual systems, based as they are on physical cards in card files, there is a tremendous pressure to assign each text to a single subject heading. In cases where this is not possible, typically one category is assigned to be primary, and the other categories are given "See Also" cards.

The Dewey decimal system was perhaps the first precoordinate system. Each document is assigned exactly one category. This is because the major purpose of the classification is to determine where to put each book on the shelves. Since books cannot be in two places at one time (unlike electronic text), they cannot be assigned two different Dewey decimal classifications. Figure 2-2 shows the major classifications of the Dewey decimal system [Grolier 85].

000-090	Generalities
100-190	Philosophy and related disciplines
200-290	Religion
300-390	Social sciences
400-490	Language
500-590	Pure sciences
600-690	Technology (applied sciences)
700-790	The arts
800-890	Literature
900-990	Geography and history

Figure 2-2: Major Divisions of the Dewey Decimal System

Of course one problem with any precoordinate system is what to do with texts that span categories. Where do books about the history of religion or the science of linguistics fit? The following query was presented to CMU's library catalog system, which uses STAIRS as its search engine:

```
[ information AND storage AND retriev$ ]
```

The search produced entries in four of the ten major categories (only one classification is given below from each major category, although there were more than 20 different numeric classifications in all). Some of these classifications get pretty deep: a number like 621.38836 separates books in that category from 100 million other categories.

070.572	Generalities
371.39445	Social Sciences
510.7855	Pure Science
621.38836	Technology

Because there were more than 20 different numeric classifications, trips to 20 different locations within the library were necessary to find all of the retrieved documents, even though the books were supposedly all about the same subject. In some systems, including the LIS-3083 library catalog here at CMU, the pre- and postcoordinate approaches are combined into a single system. For each book, report, paper or other text, the author and title are stored along with the Library of Congress subject headings for that text in a STAIRS database. Thus texts can be retrieved either by boolean keyword queries using both the words in the title and the keywords assigned by the Library of Congress.

Another example of precoordination is the coding of news stories on the Dow Jones News Service. Unlike the Dewey Decimal system where each text is assigned a single code, stories on the Dow Jones wire are assigned as many codes as are relevant to the text. The codes indicate the industry involved in the story (such as MON for monetary markets or PET for petroleum), and the names of any companies mentioned (such as BTY for British Telecom or IBM for International Business Machines, Inc.). The codes are usually assigned to a story as it is written, but before the story goes out on the news wire it is checked by a copy editor who makes any necessary formatting changes and adds any codes that have been left out during the story writing process. These copy editors have only 90 seconds to get the story out over the wire, so they do not have much time to ponder over each text.

An inherent limitation of pre-coordinated systems is the impossibility of anticipating all the possible perspectives and needs of future users. The categories and index terms chosen may abstract away an important feature needed by a future query. As time passes, the classification scheme also ages ("current events" become "history", for example), requiring changes to the classification, and a potentially huge amount of work to re-classify all of the documents in the database.

Because the knowledge representation methods for semantically based systems closely resemble the precoordinate indexing languages used by manual classification techniques, even though the semantic structures are often much more rich and expressive than individual atomic categories, it can be difficult to classify these system as either pre- or post-coordinate. To the extent that these systems manipulate their knowledge representations after the query is entered, they are post-coordinate. But the act or parsing the input text into an instantiated pattern is akin to choosing an index term from a specified list of terms, so such systems may also be viewed as precoordinate. By our "relaxed" definition, knowledge-intensive systems are pre-coordinate because the parsing step usually requires much more CPU time than the subsequent retrieval step (per text in the database). However, they use more expressive knowledge representation schemes that do not require the indexer to anticipate all future user queries.

2.3. Knowledge Rich Representations for Retrieval

This section discusses three approaches to using knowledge about natural language to aid in the retrieval process: syntactic methods, semantic methods, and case frame methods.

2.3.1. Syntactic Methods

Early artificial intelligence efforts to produce "question answering" systems used some knowledge of English syntax and semantics to retrieve information from databases in response to queries in natural language.

Raphael's SIR program for "Semantic Information Retrieval" [Raphael 68] used an internal model based on words and word associations linked in a "general manner so that no particular relations are more significant than others." Relations used were

- Set-inclusion
- Part-whole relationship
- Numeric quantity associated with the part-whole relation
- Set membership
- Left-to-right spatial relations
- Ownership

The input sentences were parsed by template matching (called "format-matching" by Raphael), with ad hoc ambiguity resolution for words such as "has":

John has a chain (ownership)

John has 5 fingers (has as parts)

Two more examples of early systems were BASEBALL [Green et al. 63], which allowed unrestricted English input about a comprehensive, static database of baseball facts, and the SAD-SAM system, "Sentence Appraiser and Diagrammer, and Semantic Analyzing Machine" [Lindsay 63]. SAD-SAM used a restricted vocabulary and grammar called "Basic English," and within this subset its performance was very good. [Sparck Jones 91] describes other early work in "classification," which developed a theory of "clumps" for describing similarities in documents based on statistical analysis of word frequencies.

An early attempt to bring more sophisticated linguistic analysis (including a comprehensive English grammar) to bear on the indexing problem was Carol Young's MYRA program [Young, C. 73]. She developed several PL/I programs that extracted syntactic information from free text, including a program that identified parts of speech of individual words, a program that recognized clause boundaries, and one that assigned case roles (derived from [Fillmore 68]) to the parts of those clauses.

Still, the trend in information retrieval has been away from linguistic analysis and towards statistics. In fact, most retrieval systems today do very little linguistic analysis of the texts they index. One limited use of syntactic analysis is to identify phrase boundaries so that more specific index terms can be built from those phrases. Phrase indexing can improve retrieval performance for concepts that are not represented by a single word. For example, if we wish to retrieve documents about *computer science*, we might try this query:

[comput$ AND science]

which would match at least the following phrases:

the computer science department

the discipline of computing science

the science of computing

but would also match across phrases, such as:

the use of computers in materials science

Just using the query:

[comput$ ADJ science]

will exclude *materials science*, but miss *science of computing*. What we really want to say is that the word "compute" must modify the word "science," so that we restrict the sciences the query should match. Determining the syntactic relation between the two words is well within the state of the art of language processing.

In particular, Fagan has investigated the use of syntactic information to identify phrases for indexing [Fagan 87a], [Fagan 87b]. He compared statistically derived indexing phrases with phrases derived using the PEG English grammar and the PLNLP programming language [Jensen 86]. He concluded that although phrases selected by using frequency and co-occurrence methods did not consistently improve retrieval performance, syntax-based selection methods can generate more useful phrases that do improve retrieval performance, by improving precision a small amount.

Evans argues that Fagan's meager performance improvement from syntactic analysis results from Fagan's failure to properly control for "noise" from the input data [Evans et al. 91]. Evans lists three sources of noise in Fagan's work:

- a limited parser unable to recognize some kinds of noun phrases,
- lack of a thesaurus to discriminate among phrases, and
- use of term-weighting on whole phrases instead of a more complicated weighting scheme that provides a compositional view of candidate terms.

Evans proposes the CLARIT system, which uses an extensive noun phrase grammar to identify candidate noun phrases as index terms. CLARIT filters the candidate noun phrases using both a thesaurus and a complicated term-weighting scheme, producing a weighted list of indexing phrases for each document. This is an intermediate approach between systems that ignore both syntax and semantics, and the semantic methods, which use syntax and semantics, but require extensive knowledge bases to parse entire sentences.

2.3.2. Semantic Methods

In contrast to systems that use only syntax to analyze a text's language, the RUBRIC retrieval system is a semantics only method for deciding whether a document is relevant to a given query [Tong et al. 86]. RUBRIC uses AND/OR trees and "fuzzy" logic to assign a degree of match to a document/query pair. The approach is to use rules that provide evidence for relevance or irrelevance. Such a system can deal with constructions that confuse syntax-only systems.

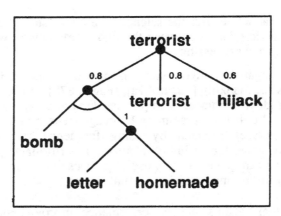

Figure 2-3: AND/OR tree for text classification

Take for example a query about terrorists (where one does not want to
retrieve stories about war). Figure 2-3 shows an AND/OR tree for a rule one
might find in a semantics-only classification system for the concept of
"terrorist." The branches of the tree are labeled with certainty factors
between 0 and 1 that indicate how strongly the subtrees are related to the root
concept. These certainty factors are assigned by the system designer (for
more information about AND/OR trees with certainty factors, see [Winston
84]). For example, using the tree shown, if a text contains the word
"terrorist" it gets an 0.8 (out of 1) score for being about terrorists. For the
word "hijack" it gets a 0.6. If it contained both terms, the score would be
combined using the rule for combining probabilities:

$$0.92 = 0.8 + 0.6 - 0.8 \times 0.6$$

The tree also matches the terms "homemade bomb" and "letter bomb," and
would assign each phrase a "terrorist" score of 0.8.

TCS is a similar semantics-mostly system for classifying stories into
multiple fixed categories [Carnegie Group 89], [Hayes, Knecht and Cellio
87]. Using pattern matching as the basic operator, the system hypothesizes
appropriate categories, and then confirms or disconfirms them based on additional rules. For example, a story like

Boston Celtics massacre Philadelphia

might be hypothesized to be either a **war**, **sports** or **disorder**, but during the
confirmation phase, an exception rule would assign the story only to the
sports category.

Such pattern matching makes for a robust system, but without more linguistic sophistication such systems cannot deal with the many different ways that an English sentence can express the same idea:

juvenile victims of crime

crime victims who are juveniles

young crime victims

A keyword or pattern based system may easily mistake any of these phrases for the concept of "juvenile criminal," and thus index into juvenile delinquency, rather than the desired category of child victims of crime.

RESEARCHER is an "Intelligent Information System" that reads textual descriptions of complex objects (in particular, patent applications) and relates them into a hierarchy in its long-term memory [Lebowitz 85a]. Because the system could relate the objects it had read about into a hierarchy, it could use the information from one text to help it understand another text. This is a significant advance, because it satisfies a basic intuition about what it means to read and understand a text — that the agent be, in some real sense, "smarter" after reading a text than before. Many systems are "smarter" in the sense that that have stored more information, but RESEARCHER takes that one step further: it not only stores more information, but it uses that information to do a better job of reading for subsequent texts. Chapter 5 describes how the FERRET system also improves its performance by use of machine learning.

RESEARCHER was a narrow system in that it dealt mainly with object descriptions and was targeted at patents. But for texts that it could understand, it provided more detailed question answering than a simple retrieval system. It could not only retrieve patent applications, but also answer questions about them by generating English descriptions of objects in the patent application database. Later versions of the program were able to tailor the output descriptions to different types of users.

2.3.3. Case Frame Methods

The most successful paradigm for natural language understanding to date has been the use of frame-based representations of knowledge, especially those derived from Fillmore's theory of case [Fillmore 68]. One of the more widely used case frame systems is Schank's *conceptual dependency theory*, often abbreviated "CD" [Schank et al. 75], [Schank & Riesbeck 81]. A con-

ceptual dependency graph is a relation between primitive objects that are
either actions, states, or noun-like "picture producers." CD theory is based
two principles [Rich 83]:

- CD representations should allow effective inference, by associat-
  ing a fixed set of inference rules with each CD primitive
- CD representations should be independent of any particular
  human language

To illustrate the first principle, if given the following sentence

John flew from Boston to New York.

one would want to be able to tell from the representation that before the
event John was in Boston and afterward he was in New York, and that the
same was true of the airplane.

To fulfill the second principle, Schank outlined a short list of primitive
actions and showed how to represent sentences as graphs built from these
primitives. For example, the CD primitive ***ptrans***, which stands for
"physical transfer," indicates motion of a physical object from one place to
another. Using Fillmore's theory of cases, the various components of the CD
graph are related using the following cases or "slots"

ACTOR	the initiating agent of an action
OBJECT	the thing affected by the action
INST	the instrument or means by the the action is effected
FROM	the source of the action
TO	the destination of the action

So our sample sentence would be represented by the following CD graph:

which literally means "John physically transferred himself from Boston to
New York using an airplane as conveyance."

No one actually draws such graphs any more. Using Lisp s-expressions, we can represent the same CD graph as a case frame:

```
(cd (actor (*john*))
    (<=>   (*ptrans*))
    (actor (*john*))
    (inst  (*airplane*))
    (from  (*boston*))
    (inst  (*new-york*))))
```

We will use the Lisp form for CD graphs throughout this dissertation. The lexical convention is to surround conceptual entries in the computer memory with asterisks (*) to differentiate them from the lexical tokens that are used by a given language to represent the concept.

CD graphs are not only independent of the surface language, they are *canonical*. Thus no matter how the sentence is phrased or what language is used, it should be represented by the same CD graph. For instance, All of the following sentences have the same CD representation as the graph given above:

John flew to New York from Boston.

John took a plan to Boston from New York.

John went from Boston to New York by Plane.

Johann von Boston nach New York ist geflogen.

This property makes CD's useful for machine translation, but it also has important implications for information retrieval. The uniqueness of the underlying representation simplifies the matching of query to text. If we wish to retrieve all documents about flying to New York, we can match the CD fragment

```
(cd (<=>   (*ptrans*))
    (inst  (*airplane*))
    (to    (*new-york*))))
```

against the CD graphs for each document. This reduces the problems of ambiguity and synonymy. Although the word "fly" is highly ambiguous in English, the CD pattern match will not retrieve stories about "house flies in Boston and New York," and will also find texts where the phrase "take a plane" is used instead of fly. Of course, this added power comes at the price of having to parse each story into case frames, and having to store these frames in addition to the text.

The first convincing demonstration that real texts covering diverse topics could be so parsed automatically was Gerald DeJong's FRUMP program [DeJong, G. 79a]. FRUMP could read and correctly understand about 10 percent of the stories on the UPI newswire, and generate short, one or two line summaries of them in five different languages. Section 3.3 contains a thorough discussion of FRUMP, and Chapter 4 describes how our research into FERRET extends the work done on FRUMP.

The RULEPAR parser developed by Jaime Carbonell at Carnegie Mellon as part of the MEDSORT project is example of case frame parsing applied to information retrieval [Carbonell & Thomason 86], [Carbonell et al. 85a]. RULEPAR combines both syntax and semantics to build case frames representing (for this particular project) the titles of medical papers about rheumatoid arthritis. FERRET uses this same kind of analysis, but where RULEPAR is a "deep" parser, FERRET is a "shallow" parser. RULEPAR attempts to understand how each word fits into each sentence, but, as will be shown in Chapter 4, FERRET's text skimming parser skips over much of its input looking for words it can understand. By giving up deep understanding, FERRET gains a compensating advantage of breadth: it is not restricted to a single, narrow domain, but can instead parse and index texts from a more than one domain at the same time (current events, astronomy, and Dow Jones).

CGI's TESS parser summarizes banking telexes and represents the result as a large case frame [Young, S. & Hayes 85]. Again, this system processes texts from a small domain, but it demonstrates the high payoff from representing documents in a effective representation such as case frames. Regardless of the phrasing used in the natural language text, the frame based representation used is the same, and the system can process that representation easily and accurately.

Dee Ann Lewis studied the relation between conceptual dependency graphs and information retrieval queries in 1984. She compared the "aboutness decisions" made by users of the DIALOG system with hand matches made by using functional relations between conceptual dependency graphs. [Lewis, D. A. E. 84]. Although the results were encouraging, David D. Lewis (no relation) concluded that the lack of precision resulting from human matching of hand-coded CD graphs was a real problem with this study [Lewis, D. D. 87]. More recent work is being undertaken at the University of Massachusetts by David D. Lewis himself. The ADRENAL project uses hand-coded frames, but real computer matching, and initial results are said to be "promising" [Croft 87], [Lewis, D. D., Croft & Bhandaru 89].

What both of these systems lack is a real text parsing component. FERRET is, therefore, a "next logical step" that attacks the question of methodological precision head-on, since FERRET both generates its own CD graphs using the MCFRUMP parser, and does its own matching with a Lisp frame matching function. The result is an effective conceptual retrieval system, as shown in Chapter 6.

2.4. Problems with the State of the Art

The existence of the NOT operator in boolean keyword query is a clue to problems with keyword based queries — it is a partially successful attempt to deal with output overload. For example, to find texts about fighting and war, but ignore texts about crime, one might try the following query:

[war AND NOT drugs]

to avoid seeing stories like

Ronald Reagan vows to step up war on drugs.

But then, of course, the following would be missed:

McNamara says we lost the Vietnam War because of drugs.

The complexity of the English language, including ambiguity, synonymy and metaphor combine to reduce the effectiveness of today's keyword-based retrieval systems.

In his keynote speech at SIGIR-85, Bruce Croft concluded that AI techniques are needed to improve information retrieval. Michael Lesk summarized his speech this way [Lesk 85]

> Bruce Croft urged AI as a way of increasing system performance, feeling
> that statistical techniques had reached their practical performance limits,
> and better performance would require specific subject domain experts to
> analyze both documents and queries.

Knowledge-based parsing can deal with some of the complexity of the language that eludes word-counting systems. But even the smartest parsers can fail when confronted by metaphor [Carbonell 82]. The AND/OR trees used by semantics-only classification systems can handle some kinds of metaphor. Hayes gives an example of metaphor that can be handled [Hayes, Knecht and Cellio 87]

The battle on center court at Wimbledon.

but he reported difficulty in handling a more extreme example

A series of battles in the disposable diaper war between Proctor and

Gamble and its competitors.

Even FRUMP had trouble with some of the stories on the UPI wire:

Ever since the dawn of pantyhose on the "unmentionable" market

killed her business, girdle designer Paula Blatt has been scheming

to make a comeback."

Summary: *Paula Blatt has been killed.*

2.5. What Kinds of Learning are Possible

As stated previously, if a system is really going to read text, then it should be smarter after it has done the reading. It should be better able to read subsequent texts—at least those about the same subject matter. Here we discuss somes systems that strive to acquire and use new information.

2.5.1. Learning Words

A fairly localized form of learning in text understanding tasks is to figure out the meaning of unknown words from surrounding context—a process that requires some comprehension of the text itself.

The FOULUP program written by Richard Granger used syntactic constraints and semantic expectations from scripts to guess the meaning of unknown words [Granger 77]. For example, in the paragraph

Friday a car swerved off Route 69. The car struck an elm.

the parser did not have the word "elm" in its lexicon. FOULUP was able to determine that an elm is a physical object from its world knowledge about car accidents.

Carbonell's POLITICS system could infer some characteristics of unknown words by applying syntactic and script level constraints, along with the assumption that the same word in other locations must also meet the constraints imposed for that context as well [Carbonell 79].

One of the most recent works is the RINA system of Zernick and Dyer than can infer the characteristics of an unknown word using generalized lexical patterns and semantic constraints of the surrounding text [Zernik & Dyer 87].

All of these systems can learn some characteristics of unknown words, and are therefore less brittle than systems than cannot handle unknown words. They also meet the criterion above that learning systems must be smarter after processing text than they were before. The FERRET system uses an on-line dictionary to deal with unknown words, as described in Section 4.4, but it could also benefit from a word learning component. In any case, it is not enough for a parser to cope with unknown words; unknown sentence constructions must also be dealt with.

2.5.2. Learning Grammar

Systems that depend on syntax for parsing must be able to cope with unknown sentence constructions. Some systems have been developed that attempt to infer new syntactic structures when faced with such difficult sentences.

The SYNNER system developed by Paul Orgren at the University of Madison-Wisconsin was able to learn an augmented transition network grammar of English by processing English sentences and their corresponding conceptual dependency graphs [Orgren 79]. The justification for giving the system both parsed and unparsed input is that in humans, vision is used in conjunction with hearing to learn language. For the machine, the conceptual dependency graph serves to convey the same meaning that a child would obtain from direct observation. Still, there is a problem in that the system can only learn syntax when some other agency is already doing the job of parsing.

William Katke developed another transition grammar learning system that did not require parsed versions of its input [Katke 85a]. Using only part-of-speech information to classify input tokens, his system developed a transition grammar from a set of training examples. Usage counts were kept on links to allow common paths through the grammar to have precedence over rare constructions. His system was able to learn grammars for subsets of English, Japanese and Chinese.

Jill Fain Lehman at Carnegie Mellon has written a command language parser called CHAMP for "Chameleonic Parser" that adapts to its users by learning new grammar rules. Using operators such as token deletion, insertion and replacement, CHAMP modifies an initial "vanilla" grammar to the style of commands actually used by the individual [Lehman 89], [Lehman & Carbonell 88].

An interesting theoretical result obtained by Berwick is that for one definition of "easily parseable," that is bounded context parseability, the resulting grammar must be "easily learnable," using the bounded degree of learning model [Berwick 84]. This is the first theoretical result towards a common assumption that human languages can be learned because they must be able to be parsed efficiently.

FERRET finesses the problem of syntax entirely. Because the MCFRUMP parser relies primarily on the meaning of the words in a sentence to parse, and only secondarily on the order in which those words appear, FERRET can often muddle through a difficult sentence and still get the right meaning, simply by fitting words together according to semantics and rejecting meaningless combinations. An example of this is shown in Section 4.1.2.

2.5.3. Learning New Concepts

The most difficult form of learning is extending the world knowledge of a system: learning new concepts. FERRET is able to exploit user feedback on its precision performance to modify its own world knowledge in an attempt to retrieve more relevant texts and fewer irrelevant ones. Chapter 5 discusses the design of FERRET's learning component, as well as describing previous work in machine learning. Chapter 6 discusses the effectiveness of FERRET's learning component and gives examples of newly learned sketchy scripts.

Chapter 3
CONCEPTUAL UNDERSTANDING OF TEXT

> To be this dumb, FRUMP actually had to be fairly smart.
> —Christopher Riesbeck

In this chapter we discuss a variety of methods for computers to understand written English text, and focus on the FRUMP parser developed at Yale by Gerald DeJong [DeJong, G. 79a].

The FRUMP parser forms the core of FERRET's text understanding ability; it was chosen over other kinds of parsers for several reasons. FRUMP demonstrated an impressive ability to read a broad class of real world texts. FRUMP's parsing "philosophy" of skimming to find the gist of a text seemed more appropriate for use in text retrieval than slower but more complete parsers. This style of parsing is also more robust, since the parser can tolerate skipping over complex material. And since it uses case-frames (in the form of CD graphs and instantiated sketchy scripts) as its output, it fits well into our model of text processing.

Although FRUMP's ability to read a broad range of newswire stories was unparalleled when it was written, we will not try to prove that it is somehow the *best* parser (whatever that might mean). We shall try instead to show in later chapters that it does a sufficiently good job of text understanding to provide better information retrieval than is possible with keyword based systems.

3.1. Natural Language Parsing

A parser is an a computer program that converts textual natural language input (which could be either a sentence from a stored text or a user query) into a structured representation that may contain syntactic or semantic information not explicitly present in the sentence itself. For indexing, we want a parser that produces a semantic representation, specifically a frame-based topic representation.

We would like a parser to be efficient, to yield a detailed, accurate representation of all the various nested relations that may be expressed in the input sentence, to be robust, so that it will recover partial information from ill-formed or obscure texts, and to be *domain independent*, so that it can process texts about many subjects, representing a wide variety of topics.

Much of the research in natural language processing is devoted to creating parsers that will perform well with respect to many of these goals; good performance with respect to all of them is at present a long-range ideal of the research. The present technology offers us a variety of parsing designs, representing various compromises. For instance, one can obtain efficiency and detail by sacrificing domain independence, and obtain robustness and detail by sacrificing domain independence and efficiency.

Perhaps the most difficult goal is domain independence. And yet this feature is critical in many realistic indexing applications. However, by sacrificing detail of representation, and by integrating techniques from *machine learning* with parsing, a compromise can be achieved that, we believe, offers considerable promise in indexing applications. For discussion of parser technology, see [Carbonell & Hayes 81], [Fain et al. 85], [Sparck Jones & Wilks 83] and [Riesbeck 82].

3.1.1. Syntax-Only Parsing

The earliest parsers did nothing more than to diagram sentences; indeed, *Webster's* dictionary defines the word ''parse'' as doing just that:

> **parse** ('pärs, 'pärz) vb. [L *pars orationis* part of speech]
> —vt. 1. to resolve (as a sentence) into component parts of
> speech and describe them grammatically 2. to describe
> grammatically by stating the part of speech and explain-
> ing the inflection and syntactical relationships —vi. 1. to
> give a grammatical description of a word or a group of
> words 2. to admit of being parsed

The complexity of the English language makes handling unrestricted textual input extremely difficult. For example, *A Grammar of Contemporary English* [Quirk et al. 72] has a 28 page index to describe the 1091 pages that describe the language.

Still, a respectable amount of the grammar for English was implemented by the Linguistic String Project at New York University [Sager 81]. Their grammar had 180 production rules with 180 restriction rules. The restriction rules contained about 1000 calls to 30 different "locating routines" that determined valid and invalid combinations of the 9,500 words in the project's lexicon. With over a decade and a half of work from many researchers, the book jacket still only describes the result as a "relatively complete grammar of English."

One of the applications of this grammar was a fact retrieval system for pediatric discharge summaries [Grishman & Hirschman 78]. This project pointed out one problem with syntax based approaches: much of what people really say or write is grammatically incorrect. The researchers had to extend their grammar to handle the sentence fragments often found in medical reports. Using the syntax-based parser as a preprocessor, they were able to write small programs that could determine, for example, whether a patient was discharged with some abnormal condition, such as a fever or a positive result from a medical test. Using a form filling technique, they assigned various parts of the sentences to columns in a table.

The form filling used in the patient discharge summary work is a symptom of another problem with syntax-only parsing: a parse tree is not an effective knowledge representation. Just knowing the subject and object of the verb does not necessarily indicate what a sentence means. To be sure, it is often easier to work from a syntax based parse than from the original sentence, and in some systems the syntax parsing is only the first of a series of processing steps. Often there is a "back-end" that converts a syntax tree into an internal form for processing. In a database query system, for example, the syntax would be mapped into the query language of the database. But different sentences with the same meaning might not be understood, because syntax alone is only an approximation to the real, underlying meaning of a sentence.

3.1.2. Semantic Grammars

One way to add meaning to a grammar is to expand the syntactic categories used into subclasses that represent the different types of objects used in the underlying system. For example, in the LADDER system, a natural language interface to a naval database, the concepts of SHIP, PORT, and GUN are represented by different production rules in the grammar, even though in a standard grammar of English they would all be just nouns. [Hendrix et al. 76]

Of course, one side-effect of adding semantics to the grammar is a huge expansion of the numbers of rules and states, with an increase in complexity and computer time used. The speed problem has been dealt with by using a "parser compiler" to transform a semantic grammar into a context free grammar [Tomita 86]. The compiler converts a smaller but slower grammar into a much larger grammar that can be parsed very quickly.

Semantic grammars are most effectively used for interface applications, because the requirements for understanding are limited in two ways. First, the amount of text actually parsed by an interface is small, a line or two per command. That means a relatively large amount of processing power can be brought to bear on the problem of understanding it. Second, if the input is too complex, grammatically incomplete, or contains unrecognized words or phrases, the person who wrote the text is right there to clarify or rephrase the message. Such luxuries do not apply to the problem of full text retrieval, since the texts are orders of magnitude larger, and the authors are not available for questioning.

3.2. Case Frames for Understanding

To really understand a text, a system must be capable of storing the meaning of that text in an effective knowledge representation. *Case frames* provide just such a solid foundation for topic representations for indexing and retrieval. The word "case" in case frames comes from Fillmore's "Case for Case" [Fillmore 68]. He showed how to describe the similarity of these sentences:

John gave the ball to mary.

The ball was given to Mary by John.

Mary was given the ball by John.

In all of these sentences, Mary is the recipient of a gift from John, and so she fills the "recipient" case of the action.

Such linguistic representations are very similar to more general frames used to represent knowledge as described by Minsky [Minsky 75]. These frames can be organized into hierarchies and networks to provide compact and effective knowledge representation. Good overviews of frame-based representations and semantic networks are given in [Brachman 79] and [Woods 75], and additional discussion can be found in [Bobrow & Winograd 77], [Carbonell 80], and [Carbonell & Joseph 85].

The basic idea is to treat a concept not as an isolated unit, but as a functional term containing "slots" that can be filled by other terms, which themselves can contain slots that are filled by terms. The ability to embed concepts in specified slots associated with other concepts provides the mechanism that is needed to represent relational information. For instance, we might distinguish the topics *juvenile victims of crime* and *juvenile criminals* (with unspecified victims) as follows:

```
(*crime*
     (victim (*human*
                    (age (*less-than* 18)))))

(*crime*
     (agent (*human*
                    (age (*less-than* 18)))))
```

These representations are organized and deployed by exploiting the subsumption of specific concepts under more general ones. For instance, we might store the information that agents of crime are human and victims of crime are human or corporate within the general concept *CRIME*. On learning that embezzlement is a crime, we do not need to add the information explicitly that the agent of embezzlement must be human; this will be computed for us by inheritance algorithms that map information from general concept to more specific subconcepts.

Frame-based systems of knowledge representation can be provided with efficient inheritance algorithms. In the simpler case in which generalizations are not allowed to have exceptions, these algorithms are efficient and relatively well understood; see, for instance, the description of KL-ONE in [Brachman 79]. The case in which exceptions are allowed is less well understood in general; but see [Touretzky 86] for recent theoretical work that provides many insights.

Some systems for representing concepts as frames have another useful property: they are *canonical*. Canonicality means that two texts with the the same meaning always map into the same frame representation. One such canonical scheme is called *conceptual dependency* (see [Schank et al. 75]), which represents events and actions with primitives such as PTRANS (physical transfer of an object) and MTRANS (mental transfer of information) and slots such as AGENT, OBJECT, and INSTRUMENT. A frame structure built with these primitives and slots is called a *conceptual dependency graph*, and there is exactly one way to represent a given concept. Thus

NASA launched Pioneer 10 to Jupiter.

Pioneer 10 was sent to Jupiter by NASA.

Sent by NASA, Pioneer 10 made its voyage to Jupiter.

Jupiter was visited by the NASA probe Pioneer 10.

are all represented by the frame (or CD graph):

```
(*ptrans*
    (agent (*nasa*)
    (object (*pioneer-spacecraft*))
    (dest (*jupiter*))
    (time (*past*)))
```

This canonical nature of such frames greatly simplifies the matching process used by an information retrieval system. This property makes the retrieval process extremely efficient, as it requires only matching the canonical representation of the user's query against the pre-coordinated canonical representations of stored documents, rather than computing related topic structures and complex mappings on the fly. Thus, if a rich representation is canonical and unambiguous, the same idea of inverted files (from instantiated canonical frames to documents) that makes current key-word retrieval so efficient can be applied to much higher quality topic representations.

To specify the concept

All spacecraft launches by NASA.

we use the pattern:

```
(*ptrans*
    (agent (*nasa*))
    (object: (*spacecraft*)))
```

which would match all four of the examples above. A corresponding keyword system would have to deal with verbs like "launch," "sent," and "visited" to achieve similar performance, querying synonym lists dynamically. However, since relations between concepts are lost, it would also retrieve stories about

NASA space experiments on Soviet launched vehicles.

on these same keywords, or worse yet, a story like

NASA probe launched by Congress.

3.2.1. Scripts for Understanding

Consider the following story:

John went into a restaurant.

He ordered a lobster.

He paid and left.

What did John eat? How do we figure out that he ate a lobster? One possibility is to build a complicated model of the goals and beliefs of John and to use this model to determine that people do not pay for food unless they like it, and if John liked the lobster he would have eaten it (unless he had to leave before he could start eating). Charles Rieger actually built an inferencer that worked this way [Schank et al. 75], but it was very slow and could not deal with very complex stories. In any event, this does not seem to be the way people understand stories like this; they do not have to work quite that hard.

One alternative is Schank's theory of scripts [Schank & Riesbeck 81]. There is an idealized restaurant script (in some Epicurean/Platonic heaven) that describes how people behave when they eat out. According to this view, events unfold in patterns, such as the following pattern:

```
$RESTAURANT
    (PERSON goes into RESTAURANT)
    (PERSON orders FOOD)
    (COOK prepares FOOD)
    (WAITER brings FOOD)
    (PERSON eats FOOD)
    (PERSON pays WAITER for FOOD)
    (PERSON leaves RESTAURANT)
```

This script allows us to handle two difficult features of language. The first is anaphora: how can we tell that "he" in the second sentence refers to "John" from the first sentence? The script gives us the answer: in the first part of the restaurant script (called a "scene" or "request"), the PERSON variable is bound to John. In the second request, "he" matches the PERSON variable, so we infer that John was the person who did the ordering.

The second feature is implicit communication. The third sentence in our story matches the last two requests from the script. In the absence of disconfirming information, we assume that the track of the script was followed properly. Thus we assume that the lobster was cooked, that a waiter brought John the lobster, and that John ate the lobster.

A parser based on this idea called SAM (for Script Applier Mechanism) was built by Richard Cullingford [Schank & Riesbeck 81]. SAM could handle more complex situations (if it had the necessary script), but SAM required CPU time proportional to the number of scripts in its database. Thus as it got smarter it also got slower.

3.3. FRUMP

Gerald DeJong's FRUMP was an answer to the speed versus power problem. By clever use of data structures, FRUMP was able to do script base processing of inputs in time logarithmically related to the number of scripts in its database, and as a result it was very fast. FRUMP would "skim" its input texts to determine their main themes without slogging through each and every word [DeJong, G. 79a]. Frump successfully analyzed 10% of the news stories on the UPI newswire, requiring an average of 20 seconds per story. DeJong claimed that Frump is theoretically capable of understanding 50% of the UPI wire. "Successful" here means that it correctly understood the main theme of the text — some stories were not understood because although Frump correctly found the subthemes, it did not correctly identify the main point. Others failed because Frump misinterpreted the actions in the story, or simply lacked the necessary information to process the story.

FRUMP's understanding of a text is based on "sketchy scripts," which are simpler than other script-based natural language programs. Frump is composed of two main modules: the *predictor*, which uses the script to constrain the meaning of the input, and the *substantiator*, which uses those constraints to analyze the text. Although Frump is fundamentally top-down (predict then substantiate) there is also a bottom-up component to the analysis (mainly for proper script selection).

3.3.1. Text Skimming

Webster's defines skimming as

> **skim**[1] ('skim) vb. **skimmed skim·ming** [ME *skimmen*] —vt. 2. to read, study, or examine superficially and rapidly; *specif* :: to glance through (as a book) for the chief ideas or the plot

FRUMP uses a top-down, tree-based approach to find the basic idea of its input text. The resulting parser is very fast, because it does not try to find every possible meaning of a text. Instead the parser is always seeking to confirm a top-down expectation based on the scripts available to the system. Figure 3-1 shows an input text parsed by FRUMP taken from DeJong's thesis. Only the underlined words were used by the parser to construct its summary, everything else was skipped.

```
UPI Story 4, December 5, 1978

INPUT:

    COLORADO (UPI)-RESCUERS ON SNOWCATS
PUSHED THROUGH FIVE-FOOT SNOWDRIFTS TO
REACH THE WRECKAGE OF A TWINENGINE ROCKY
MOUNTAIN AIRWAYS PLANE THAT CRASHED IN
COLORADO'S RUGGED BUFFALO PASS. AUTHORITIES
REPORTED ONE PERSON HAD BEEN KILLED BUT
THAT 21 OTHERS ABOARD SURVIVED. AMBULANCES
WERE ORDERED TO REMOVE THEM FROM THE
WILDERNESS.

CPU TIME FOR UNDERSTANDING = 2470 MILLISECONDS
ENGLISH SUMMARY:

    A VEHICLE ACCIDENT OCCURRED IN COLORADO.
A PLANE HIT THE GROUND.  1 PERSON DIED.
```

Figure 3-1: Sample Input Story for FRUMP

The conceptual representation of the summary is given in Figure 3-2. The notation has been changed from the original FRUMP format to the case-frame style used by FERRET, but the mapping is straight-forward. The first two frames are the instantiated sketchy scripts that were satisfied, and the last two frames are the corresponding conceptual dependency graphs built by the parser.

DeJong points out two features of this example. First, note that the parser has to infer that the plane hit the ground, because the ground is not explicitly mentioned in the story. For information retrieval, that means that it can be

```
($vehicle-accident
   (&obj1 (*plane*))
   (&obj2 (*ground*))
   (loc (*colorado*)))

(|casualty
   (&deadgrp (*human* (quant (1)))
   (&hurtgrp nil)
   (&missinggrp nil))

(cd
   (actor (*plane*))
   (<=> (*propel*))
   (object (*ground*))
   (loc (*colorado*))
   (manner (*violent*)))

(cd
   (actor (*human* (quant (1))))
   (is (*health* (value (-10)))))
```

Figure 3-2: FRUMP's output

possible to retrieve on story elements that are not explicitly present in the text. Such matches improve the recall performance of the IR system.

Second, the summary produced is not merely a representative sentence chosen from the text. For example, simply choosing the first sentence of the text would omit the fact that one person was killed, and include unnecessary details about the height of the snow. Excluding such details can improve the precision of the retrieval system, because matches are more likely to be found based on the main point of the text, rather than on a word or phrase that is not directly relevant to the story.

For example, given a query to find airplane crashes caused by icing, a word based approach is likely to retrieve this story, because the words "snow" and "crash" appear in the same sentence, even though there is no reason to infer such a cause from the text.

3.3.2. The Predictor and the Substantiator

One innovation of the FRUMP parser is that it breaks the parsing problem into two parts in such a way that neither component is required to deal with the whole text at once. This is in contrast to earlier parsers that were divided into steps such as syntactic, semantic and pragmatic. The older style of parsing meant that the syntax component might spend much of its time building up a complete interpretation of the input, and only later would the semantic component discover that that particular interpretation was meaningless.

Instead, FRUMP is split into a "predictor" and a "substantiator." The predictor uses a discrimination tree (described later) to propose a particular slot filler for a frame, and the substantiator used inference and textual analysis to confirm or disconfirm the proposed slot fillers. Before describing each component in detail, we will see roughly how FRUMP parses the sample story above:

1. The parser scans left to right trying to find a structure building word (usually a verb). "Push" is such a word, but the partial structure built by "push" cannot be extended, so that path dies.

2. The word "crashed" is the next structure building word, and it builds the following partial conceptual dependency graph:

   ```
   (cd
         (<=> (*propel*))
         (manner (*violent*)))
   ```

3. Once a partial structure has been started, the top-down component can direct the rest of the processing. The next step is to locate an actor for the *PROPEL* action. The predictor generates a request to fill the ACTOR slot with one of a long list of fillers (*VEHICLE*, *HUMAN*, *MILITARY-UNIT*, ...). This request is passed to the substantiator.

4. The substantiator has a request to find a noun matching one element of the possible filler list. The slot to be filled is also indicated: the actor. Since the verb is in active voice, the actor must be in the subject position, before the verb. A scan backwards find the word "plane," which according to the type hierarchy can be a type of vehicle. So the partial CD graph is extended to be:

```
(cd
    (actor (*plane*))
    (<=> (*propel*))
    (manner (*violent*)))
```

5. There are only two scripts that match this partial CD, one for a vehicle hitting a person, and one for a vehicle hitting a physical object. So the predictor requests that the OBJECT slot be filled with one of (*HUMAN*, *PHYSOBJ*).

6. The substantiator is requested to fill the object slot, so it looks immediately after the verb to locate the direct object. This scan is terminated immediately by the preposition "in," so the textual analysis fails to find an object. The substantiator has a rule, however, that allows it to infer that the object is the ground since the MANNER of the PROPEL action is violent. The inference is marked with a confidence factor less than certainty, and graph is extended as follows:

```
(cd
    (actor (*plane*))
    (<=> (*propel*))
    (object (*ground*))
    (manner (*violent*)))
```

7. Where before there were two possible matching scripts, there is now only one, the $VEHICLE-ACCIDENT script for a vehicle hitting a physical object. This script is selected, and the scripts variables &OBJ1 and &OBJ2 are bound to *PLANE* and *GROUND* respectively.

8. Once the script is selected, any optional slots, such as the location of the action, are searched for. FRUMP also has a higher level of episodic knowledge called "issue skeletons" to connect scripts together, and to allow one script to suggest that another script might be appropriate. In this example the vehicle accident script also activates the casualty script, which is used to find that one person died in the accident.

This example shows the back and forth cooperation between the two major parts of FRUMP. As the conceptual representation grows from the kernel built from the verb, the predictor says "look here for one of these" and the substantiator says "I looked there and I found this thing that can be one of those." This organization finesses one of the trickiest problems in parsing and retrieval: ambiguity.

Take the word "plane" in the above story. It can have at least six different meanings:

- to make smooth or even
- a plant of the genus *Platanus*
- a tool for shaping wood
- a flat or level surface
- an airplane
- to skim across the surface of a body of water

But the predictor asks "is there a vehicle in the subject position?", so the substantiator must merely answer the question "can a plane be a vehicle?" The other meanings of the word are never considered, and therefore do not slow the parser down.

On retrieval, the airplane meaning of the word is stored in the abstract. Thus the other meanings do not interfere with retrieval. This can improve precision, because queries about "wood carving tools" do not retrieve this story about a plane crash. Recall can also be improved, because queries about "vehicle accidents" do retrieve this story, even though neither the word "vehicle" or "accident" appears.

3.3.3. Script Selection

One of the problems with a script based understanding system is knowing which script to use to understand a given text. SAM, for example, simply tried each script in turn, matching them against parses of the sentences in the story that were built by another parser such as ELI (English Language Interpreter, see [Schank & Riesbeck 81]). This approach had two problems. One was that the scripts could not be used in the initial parsing process, but only for the later processing of the individual sentences into a coherent unit. The other was that the script application process require time proportional to the number of possible scripts. In a system with enough scripts to cover a broad range of topics, SAM would simply be too slow.

One suggestion was to tie each script to a suggestive word: the restaurant script might be activated upon seeing words like "restaurant," "waiter", "food" or "order." But such a scheme would necessarily waste time on sentences like:

A bomb exploded outside a French restaurant today.

and night miss other sentences like

John asked for some take-out Chinese.

FRUMP solves both of these problems by using a data structure called a "Sketchy Script Initiator Discrimination Tree" or SSIDT, which is compiled from all of the available scripts in a system. The SSIDT classifies the key portions of each script by its CD primitive or ACTION, ACTOR, OBJECT and so on. A portion of this tree is shown in Figure 3-3.

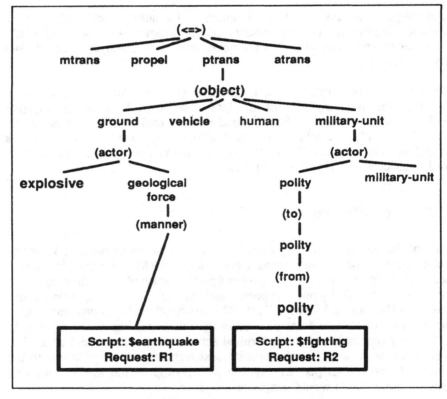

Figure 3-3: Portion of an SSIDT

For example if the verb indicates physical movement (such as "send"), then the *PTRANS* branch is taken. Then the predictor can determine that the actor should be one of GEOLOGICAL-FORCE, HUMAN, POLITY, or

MILITARY-UNIT. Assuming that the actor is "United States," a polity, then that branch is followed. The substantiator is required only to determine whether any member of a list can be found in the subject position. The choices for the OBJECT slot are then only MILITARY-UNIT and HUMAN. In one case, the action is likely to be either an invasion or troop reinforcement, and both of these lead to the $FIGHTING script. If the OBJECT is a human, then it might be some kind of state visit, covered by the $MEETING script.

By using a tree structure, FRUMP is able to home in on the correct script in logarithmic time rather than linear time, and so it can still function even with a very large number of possible scripts. Too, FRUMP can use the knowledge implicit in the scripts to assist in the actual textual analysis, so ambiguous word senses are never even considered, unless they are relevant. And since the correct script is invoked based on the conceptual representation of the sentence, no appeal to highly loaded words like "earthquake" or "invasion" is needed to activate the script.

3.3.4. Limitations

The use of sketchy scripts in FRUMP is not without its problems. DeJong lists three limitations of his original program:

- Lack of a necessary script.
- Undefined vocabulary words.
- Unknown/complex sentence structure.

Chapter 4 will discuss how FERRET deals with the lack of vocabulary. Chapter 5 will discuss how FERRET deals with missing scripts. FERRET is no better than FRUMP at dealing with unusual sentence structure, and this can lead to difficulty. Consider the following actual example, taken from [Riesbeck 82]:

Pope's death shakes the Western Hemisphere.

to which FRUMP gave this summary:

```
There was an earthquake in the Western Hemisphere.
The Pope died.
```

Knowing how FRUMP works to understand a sentence, we can see how it misunderstood this example. The Western Hemisphere is a physical location, and it was moving cyclically, so there must have been an earthquake. Natural disasters like earthquakes often have casualties, and we find that indeed, the Pope has died.

On the positive side, FRUMP did catch on to the fact that the Pope died, and in a retrieval system, a query about papal deaths would have retrieved this story correctly. Of course, the misunderstanding would lead to reduced precision if the query were about earthquakes in the Western Hemisphere. But in the information retrieval context, we need not hold the parser to quite as high a standard of excellence as we might for a machine translation or summarization system. If the retrieval finds the story when it should, we can forgive a little bit of creative misunderstanding.

Chapter 4
THE FERRET SYSTEM

I'll fer him, and firk him, and ferret him.
—William Shakespeare
Henry V, Act IV, Scene 4

This chapter describes the architecture and components of the FERRET retrieval system, except for the script learning component, which is discussed in Chapter 5.

4.1. Architectural Overview

The FERRET information retrieval architecture shown in Figure 4-1 consists of three major components:

- The text parser
- The query parser
- The case frame matcher

The query parser is not currently implemented, but is instead simulated by the text parser and a small post-processing function. For more discussion of the requirements of a real query parser, see Section 7.3.1. In addition to these, there is a very simple user interface that allows the user to interrogate the FERRET database and retrieve texts. The interface is really just the visible part of a huge iceberg.

The text parser is like the rest of the iceberg: it's big and slow and mostly invisible. Its job is to read incoming stories from NETNEWS and convert them into symbolic representations called "abstracts" that are stored in an "abstract database." Two kinds of objects are produced that are called "abstracts": the first is the instantiated sketchy script, and the second is the actual CD graph that matches the script. The core of the parser is called MCFRUMP, because it is a reimplementation of the FRUMP parser. Some of

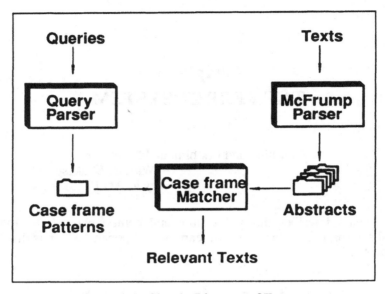

Figure 4-1: Simple Diagram of FERRET

the complexity of FRUMP is gone, and three new components have been added, a lexical scanner that preprocesses the text, an interface to *Webster's Seventh Dictionary* and a script learning component. The MCFRUMP parser is described in Section 4.3, the scanner in Section 4.2 and the dictionary interface in Section 4.4. The script learning component has its own chapter, Chapter 5.

The query parser performs a similar task for queries to the database, producing ''abstract patterns'' that match the abstracts from the text parser. This is the part that does not exist; but is reserved for future work. Currently, all queries are entered directly as partial CD graphs or partial instantiated sketchy scripts built by the simulated parser. See Section 7.3 for more discussion.

The case frame matcher brings the two parsers together, determining whether a given abstract pattern matches a specific abstract. Since boths the instantiated sketchy script and the CD graph are case frames, the matcher has a relatively simple task to match each frame slot-for-slot and each filler by checking the type hierarchy. The matcher is described in Section 4.5.

4.1.1. The Relevance Homomorphism Assumption

The simple design shown in Figure 4-1 is based on the assumption that human judgments about the relevance of a text to a query are approximated by the process of parsing both the query and the text into a computer knowledge representation and then matching the two representations. These operations of parsing and case frame matching form a homomorphism as shown in Figure 4-2.

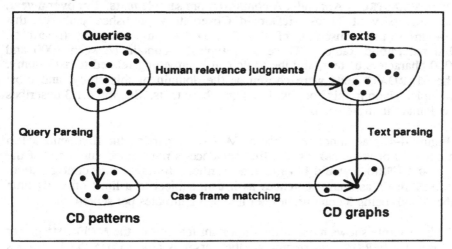

Figure 4-2: Relevance Homomorphism Assumption

We can restate the goal of better parsing from Section 1.6.4 in terms of this assumption: CD parsing and case frame matching approximate human judgments more closely than word counting and frequency matching. FERRET is a concrete example of a computer program that demonstrates these operations in practice.

Note that the mappings from query to CD pattern and text to CD are many-to-one. This is a consequence of choosing a canonical knowledge representation. This uniqueness property greatly simplifies the matching process, or perhaps a more fair statement is that it improves the accuracy of matching for a given level of simplicity.

4.1.2. A Sample Text Being Parsed

Before diving into an exposition about each of the various pieces of code, we present two examples. Here we show a sample text from the USENET SCI.ASTRO newsgroup, and show how the text parser reads and represents the text. In the next section we show a sample retrieval.

Figure 4-3 shows a text taken from the USENET Astronomy newsgroup called SCI.ASTRO.[*] Appendix A contains more sample texts. For over a year, the University of Texas McDonald Observatory published daily on this newsgroup the transcripts of the STARDATE radio program (heard on National Public Radio). These texts typically contain between 1000 and 2000 characters of text, and the topic can be anything related to astronomy. The STARDATE texts were chosen as the domain of this study, and most examples given in this book will be from these texts. Section 6.1.3 describes the domain in more detail.

Figure 4-4 is an annotated trace of MCFRUMP parsing the first sentence in this text. For some stories, the first sentence is not a good summary of the text, and FERRET would have to read further. In its current configuration, FERRET reads as many sentences as it can, subject to a limit on CPU time (the default being 8 cpu minutes per text and 3 minutes per sentence).[*]

This example shows most of the important features of the MCFRUMP parser as used by FERRET. In particular, the parser is able to use the *Webster's* dictionary to understand a previously unknown verb. Even though the word is ambiguous, the parser uses the constraints from its database of scripts to select the correct meaning of the new word, and correctly parses the sentence. Because the parser is semantically oriented, rather than syntactically, it is not confused by the complicated structure of the sentence:

X was the first Y to Z into W

is successfully understood as

X Z' ed into W

---

[*]At that time, the Astronomy newsgroup was called NET.ASTRO. The names of the newsgroups were completely reorganized on October 12, 1986.

[*]These times were appropriate for a MicroVax II running Franz Lisp. Typical sentences are parsed in between 1 and 2 minutes of cpu time.

```
Article 1307 of 1351, Mar  3 02:00.
Subject: StarDate: March 3 Pioneer 10
From: dipper@utastro
Organization: U. Texas, Astronomy, Austin, TX
Newsgroups: net.astro
Date: Mon, 3-Mar-86 02:00:18 EST

Pioneer 10 was the first spacecraft to venture into the
outer solar system.  More -- coming up.

March 3  Pioneer 10

On today's date in the year 1972, NASA's Pioneer 10 spacecraft was
launched toward the outer solar system.  It was to become the first
craft to travel beyond the asteroid belt -- and the first to
encounter mighty Jupiter.

Pioneer 10 is now on its way out of the solar system.  It is now
farther from the sun than any of the known planets -- still
sampling the environment through which it moves -- and still
transmitting data back to Earth.

The spacecraft was originally designed for a mission lasting 21
months.  Its primary mission was to encounter Jupiter.

But the spacecraft has done much more.  Scientists used Pioneer 10
data to go beyond the previous picture of the solar system -- that
of a central sun surrounded by a flat disk of planets.  Thanks to
Pioneer 10, we can now envision a huge magnetic bubble containing
the planets and sun -- a bubble that may be streamlined into a
teardrop as the sun at its heart moves through the galaxy.  Some
scientists also think this bubble "breathes" -- expands and
contracts -- with each 11-year cycle of activity on the sun.

The outer boundary of the bubble is known as the heliopause, the
end of the sun's influence.  Outside the heliopause lies the
unsampled gas and dust of interstellar space.  Although no one
knows exactly when it will happen, Pioneer 10 will be the first
craft from Earth to cross the heliopause -- and venture into the
galaxy at large.

Script by Deborah Byrd.
(c) Copyright 1985, 1986 McDonald Observatory,
University of Texas at Austin
```

Figure 4-3: A Sample STARDATE Text

```
% special pioneer.txt | scan >
  pioneer.scn
Scanned pioneer.txt, 44 lines, 0.78
  seconds.
Scanned stdin, 30 lines, 1.38 seconds.
```

First the article is run through two LEX scanning programs that handle some simple lexical conventions. The SCAN program picks out USENET message headers, numbers and dates. The SPECIAL program handles more exotic items such as phone numbers, electronic mail addresses, latitudes and longitudes, and stellar positions. These are converted into special canonical forms that simplify later Lisp processing.

```
% mcfrump
McFrump, 15-May-88, from Franz Lisp,
  Opus 38

1.run-mcfrump pioneer.scn

Processing article (%cpt stardate
  %colon %cpt march 3 %cpt pioneer 10)
```

File PIONEER.SCN contains the output from the text scanner.

```
Working on article (reference (file
  pioneer.txt) (line 1) (byte 0))
[ Processing phrases ]
[ Finding sentence breaks ]
Initial processing time: 15.16
```

Each article is marked by its file and byte position within the file. This identification is used by the retrieval interface to display the original text after an article is retrieved.

```
Sentence: (p-258 pioneer-spacecraft was
  the first spacecraft to venture into
  the outer solar-system %period)
```

This is the sentence after it has been scanned and the phrases have been collapsed. The P-258 is a paragraph marker from the scanner indicating that this sentence starts at byte 258 in the text file. The tokens PIONEER-SPACECRAFT and SOLAR-SYSTEM have been recognized and collapsed by phrase rules stored under the words ''pioneer'' and ''solar'' during the first phase of processing the article.

```
[ p-258, index=1 ]
[ pioneer-spacecraft, index=2 ]
[ was, index=3 ]
[ the, index=4 ]
[ first, index=5 ]
[ spacecraft, index=6 ]
[ to, index=7 ]
```

McFRUMP first scans left-to-right searching for a word that builds a partial concept. These are usually verbs. The partial concept includes at least a CD primitive and sometimes one or more specific slot fillers.

Figure 4-4: Annotated Trace of a Sample Parser Run

```
[ venture, index=8 ]
Looking for 'venture' in webster's...
Looking for 'despite' in webster's...
Using defn of venture => advance1
    (to proceed despite danger %colon
    %colon dare)

Using defn of venture => offer1
Using defn of venture => offer3
    (to offer at the risk of rebuff
    %comma rejection %comma or censure)

******* venture (offer3) builds:
    (cd (<=> (*mtrans*))
        (mobject (*concept*
                        (type (*offer*)))))
```

Notice that "venture" is not in the lexical knowledge base, but *Webster's* lists three definitions that are partial synonyms for words that are in the knowledge base. The word "despite" appears in one definition of "venture," and this causes a recursive inquiry to *Webster's*. The complete definition of "venture" is shown in Figure A-13 in Appendix A.4.

```
Climb: 'actor' slot of
    (cd (<=> (*mtrans*))
        (mobject (*concept*
                        (type
    (*offer*)))))
Trying to fill 'actor' with one of
(*worker-kind* *polity* *human*
    *authorities* *organization* *higher-
    animate*)
Optimized filler list (*higher-
    animate*)
```

Two of the definitions in *Webster's* are near-synonyms of words in McFRUMP's lexicon, and there are three words senses for them. One is "advance" and two are "offers." The last of these, a type of offer, is popped off a stack and creates this piece of CD graph, which translates roughly as "transmitting a proposal."

Following the *MTRANS* branch of the SSIDT, the parser tries first to find an agent for the *MTRANS* action. As a speed enhancement done only for the actor slot, the possible categories words to the left of the verb have been intersected with the list of fillers, and that reduces to *HIGHER-ANIMATE*.

```
Found subject (spacecraft1 6 nil subj)
Found more specific filler for
    *spacecraft* => (*pioneer-
    spacecraft*)
Parse Rule 2 fills 'actor' with
    (*pioneer-spacecraft*)
```

The parser scans right-to-left starting just before the verb, and finds "spacecraft." The type hierarchy lists a spacecraft as a vehicle, which can act as a higher-animate, so *PIONEER-SPACECRAFT* is acceptable as the actor for this script. The anaphora handling routine finds a more specific spacecraft earlier in the same sentence, and assigns it to be the slot filler.

```
Climb: 'to' slot of
    (cd (<=> (*mtrans*))
        (mobject (*concept*
                        (type (*offer*))))
        (actor (*pioneer-spacecraft*)))
Trying to fill 'to' with one of (nil
    *higher-animate*)
```

The *OUTER-SOLAR-SYSTEM* is not a higher-animate, and therefore cannot act as the recipient of a proposal. Therefore this path is a dead-end and is removed.

Figure 4-4 (cont)

```
******* venture (offer1) builds:

        ...trace omitted...

******* venture (advance1) builds:
  (cd (<=> (*ptrans*)))

Climb: 'actor' slot of (cd (<=>
  (*ptrans*)))
Trying to fill 'actor' with one of
(*spacecraft* *outer-space-object*
  *polity* *natural-force* *combustion*
  *organization* *geo-force* *human-
  def* nil *water* *criminal-type*
  *human*)
Optimized filler list (*spacecraft*)

Found subject (spacecraft1 6 nil subj)
Found more specific filler for
  *spacecraft* => (*pioneer-
  spacecraft*)
Parse Rule 2 fills 'actor' with
  (*pioneer-spacecraft*)

Climb: 'object' slot of (cd (<=>
  (*ptrans*)))
Trying to fill 'object' with one of
  (*human-def*)




Climb: 'object' slot of
  (cd (<=> (*ptrans*))
      (actor (*pioneer-spacecraft*)))
Trying to fill 'object' with one of
  (*human-def*)

Climb: 'object' slot of
  (cd (<=> (*ptrans*))
      (actor (*pioneer-spacecraft*)))
Trying to fill 'object' with one of
  (*spacecraft*)
Parse Rule 1 fills 'object' with
  (*pioneer-spacecraft*)
```

The second sense of the word "offer" is processed just like OFFER3, and that path also dies.

The word "venture" is defined in *Webster's* "to proceed," which in McFRUMP has a word sense ADVANCE1. This word was originally used by FRUMP to understand stories about troop movements and attacks. But in combination with *Webster's* this knowledge is used to understand a sentence from a totally different domain.

The parser again finds *PIONEER-SPACECRAFT* as a filler for the ACTOR slot. Note that this time the parser is looking for a spacecraft rather than a higher-animate. This part of the discrimination tree was built by the $LAUNCH script.

There are multiple scripts that are based on *PTRANS*, in particular the $MEET script has requests for particular people like ambassadors travelling to other countries. Since competing partial parses are handled with a breadth-first search, this meaning is tried before the parser attempts to extend the $LAUNCH meaning of the sentence. Of course, since there is no person mentioned in the sentence, this path dies too.

This is another version of the $MEET interpretation, which fails.

Now the parser tries to extend the partial concept built by the $LAUNCH script. The inference code decides that the Pioneer spacecraft is object of the *PTRANS* as well as the actor.

Figure 4-4 (cont)

```
Climb: 'to' slot of
    (cd (<=> (*ptrans*))
        (actor (*pioneer-spacecraft*))
        (object (*pioneer-
spacecraft*)))
Trying to fill 'to' with one of
    (*outer-space-location*)
Parse Rule 2 fills 'to' with
    (*solar-system* (type (w7-outer))
    (ref (def)))

Accepting script
    (launch-r2
        (&spacecraft
            (*pioneer-spacecraft*))
        (&launch-dest
            (*solar-system*
                (type (w7-outer))
                (ref (def)))))

    (cd
        (<=> (*ptrans*))
        (actor (*pioneer-spacecraft*))
        (object (*pioneer-spacecraft*))
        (to (*solar-system*
                (type (w7-outer))
                (ref (def)))))

Parsing time: 107.03 seconds
```

To activate the $LAUNCH script, the destination is needed, and it must be an outer space location. In the phrase "the outer solar system," the words "solar system" are combined by the phrase handling rules, and the word outer is found in *Webster's*. Although the parser has no specific meaning for "outer," it finds the part-of-speech is adjective, and so the token W7-OUTER is added to the conceptual filler *SOLAR-SYSTEM*.

The parser now has everything it needs to activate the $LAUNCH script, and stores both the instantiated script and the CD graph in the abstract database as indices to this text. Since no source is mentioned in the sentence, the FROM slot of the graph is left unfilled. The original FRUMP had a much more powerful inference capability, and would have been able to assume that the launch must have come from the United States (or at least the planet Earth). MCFRUMP is a simpler parser in this respect.

This time was obtained on an unloaded MicroVax II running Franz Lisp, Opus 38. MCFRUMP is not as fast as the original FRUMP, because of the breadth-first search for concepts. Unlike FRUMP, MCFRUMP can find multiple interpretations for ambiguous sentences, and uses both meanings to index the text for retrieval, potentially reducing precision, but increasing recall. This flexibility comes at the expense of a slower parser.

Figure 4-4 (cont)

4.1.3. A Sample Query Being Matched

Figures 4-5 and 4-6 show two very similar queries to the retrieval system, both of which match the text parsed in the previous example. Figure 4-7 shows the abstract that matched both queries. In the first case, in Figure 4-5, the user starts the retrieval system by typing **(ferret)**, and is then asked to type a CD pattern. The user types **(launch-r2)**, which specifies that all examples of the $LAUNCH script, request number 2, are to be retrieved. Thirteen articles are matched, and the user is presented with a list of titles and matching sentences. When the user types just the number of the article, the full text of the article is popped up on the screen in a separate editor window.

The matching sentences shown are the results of the phrase processing phase, so there are some oddities. For example, the words "the planet Uranus" are collapsed to "the Uranus," since "planet Uranus" is mapped simply to "Uranus." Similarly, the times and dates have been collapsed to tokens from the original words like "yesterday" or "tomorrow."

Figure 4-6 shows how the retrieval can be based on a complete or partial CD graph. The pattern used is

```
(cd (<=> (*ptrans*))
    (object (*spacecraft*))
    (to (*outer-space-location*)))
```

Asks for all examples of spacecraft travelling to any place in outer space. This one query matches our sample text, and retrieves fifteen texts in all. That is two more than the previous query, because some of the stories found were instances of the $LAUNCH-R1 script or the $SPACETRAVEL script instead of $LAUNCH-R2. The actual abstract that was matched by both queries is shown in Figure 4-7.

Phrasing the same query as a boolean combination of keywords would be very difficult, and would likely miss our sample text. No reasonable list of verbs for launching spacecraft would include "venture."

```
Ferret,   2-May-88, from Franz Lisp, Opus 38

1.ferret

                    Top level interface to Ferret

Enter CD pattern: (launch-r2)

[ Found 13 articles ]

Articles matching (launch-r2)

    1] StarDate: January 5  On the Way to the Heliopause
       ((Only 4 spacecraft from Earth have ever gone toward
         the outer solar-system -- toward the giant planets
         Jupiter %c Saturn %c Uranus and Neptune)
        (and the Voyagers one and 2 %c will also become the
         first craft from Earth to cross the heliopause --
         the boundary between the realm of sol and the wide
         open spaces of the galaxy at large)
        (no-one knows when these craft will cross the
         heliopause %c))
    2] StarDate: February 24  Eleven Months to Uranus
       ((It will be a relatively old spacecraft that encounters
         the uranus next year))
    3] StarDate: March 24  Ten Months to Uranus
       ((voyager-probe will encounter the uranus exactly 10
         months from time-march-24-1985))
    4] StarDate: June 24  Seven Months to Uranus
       ((When the voyager-probe encounters Uranus %c that
         outer world will have just come back to our predawn
         sky))
    5] StarDate: August 25  On To Neptune
       ((time-august-24-1985 we talked about the upcoming
         voyager-probe encounter with the uranus -- due to
         take place this coming winter)
        (But if it survives past the encounter with Uranus
         %c it will go on to encounter Neptune))
```

Figure 4-5: Sample Retrieval by Script

```
  6] StarDate: September 10   I.C.E. Encounters Giacobini-
     Zinner
     ((No spacecraft has ever encountered a comet))
  7] StarDate: November 17   The Gossamer Ring of Jupiter
     ((When the voyager-probe passed by Jupiter in 0 it sent
       back of images of the largest planet in our solar-
       system %c))
  8] StarDate: January 23   Voyager and Uranus
     ((Voyager is the first spacecraft to visit the ordinal-7
       planet outward from sol))
  9] StarDate: March 3   Pioneer 10
     ((pioneer-spacecraft was the first spacecraft to venture
       into the outer solar-system))
 10] StarDate: September 3   Highway to Space
     ((A spaceship that cycles continuously between the orbits
       of Mars and the Earth))
 11] StarDate: March 8   Jupiter's Moon Io
     ((It was Voyager is encounter with Jupiter -- and the
       spacecraft was taking a longer-than-usual exposure
       of the jovian moon Io))
 12] StarDate: September 2   A Look at the Planet Neptune
     ((The voyager-probe will encounter the neptune in 1989)
      (It will encounter Neptune on time-august-24-1987))
 13] StarDate: October 14   Galileo at Jupiter
     ((The next spacecraft to visit Jupiter is scheduled to
       arrive a decade and half after Voyager -- in the year
       1995))

Choice (or 'q' to quit): 9
[ Use the editor to see f500/star.8603, line 39.
  Type ^C to return ]
```

...the article is popped up in a separate window...

Figure 4-5: Sample Retrieval by Script - Cont.

```
Enter CD pattern: (cd (<=> (*ptrans*)) (object (*spacecraft*))
                      (to (*outer-space-location*)))

[ Found 15 articles ]

Articles matching
  (cd (<=> (*ptrans*))
      (object (*spacecraft*))
      (to (*outer-space-location*)))

  1] StarDate: January 5  On the Way to the Heliopause
     ((Only 4 spacecraft from Earth have ever gone toward
       the outer solar-system -- toward the giant planets
       Jupiter %c Saturn %c Uranus and Neptune)
      (and the Voyagers one and 2 %c will also become the
       first craft from Earth to cross the heliopause --
       the boundary between the realm of sol and the wide
       open spaces of the galaxy at large)
      (no-one knows when these craft will cross the
       heliopause %c))
  2] StarDate: February 24  Eleven Months to Uranus
     ((It will be a relatively old spacecraft that
       encounters the uranus next year))
  3] StarDate: March 24  Ten Months to Uranus
     ((voyager-probe will encounter the uranus exactly 10
       months from time-march-24-1985))
  4] StarDate: June 24  Seven Months to Uranus
     ((When the voyager-probe encounters Uranus %c that
       outer world will have just come back to our
       predawn sky))
  5] StarDate: August 25  On To Neptune
     ((time-august-24-1985 we talked about the upcoming
       voyager-probe encounter with the uranus -- due to
       take place this coming winter)
      (But if it survives past the encounter with Uranus
       %c it will go on to encounter Neptune))
  6] StarDate: September 10  I.C.E. Encounters
                   Giacobini-Zinner
     ((No spacecraft has ever encountered a comet))
  7] StarDate: November 17  The Gossamer Ring of Jupiter
     ((When the voyager-probe passed by Jupiter in 0 it
       sent back of images of the largest planet in our
       solar-system %c))
  8] StarDate: January 23  Voyager and Uranus
     ((Voyager is the first spacecraft to visit the
       ordinal-7 planet outward from sol))
  9] StarDate: March 3  Pioneer 10
     ((pioneer-spacecraft was the first spacecraft to
       venture into the outer solar-system))
```

Figure 4-6: Sample Retrieval by CD graph

```
10] StarDate: April 24  The Fifth Nation in Space
    ((It was on time-april-24-1970 that the first
      Chinese satellite was placed in orbit))
11] StarDate: September 3  Highway to Space
    ((A spaceship that cycles continuously between the
      orbits of Mars and the Earth))
12] StarDate: March 8  Jupiter's Moon Io
    ((It was Voyager is encounter with Jupiter -- and
      the spacecraft was taking a longer - than - usual
      exposure of the jovian moon Io))
13] StarDate: April 19  The First -- and Seventh --
                        Salyuts
    ((It was the first in a series of small space
      stations placed into orbit by the Soviets))
14] StarDate: September 2  A Look at the Planet Neptune
    ((The voyager-probe will encounter the neptune in
      1989)
     (It will encounter Neptune on time-august-24-1987))
15] StarDate: October 14  Galileo at Jupiter
    ((The next spacecraft to visit Jupiter is scheduled
      to arrive a decade and half after Voyager -- in
      the year 1995))
```

Figure 4-6: Sample Retrieval by CD graph

```
Choice (or 'q' to quit): a 9

Abstract: ((reference (file f500/star.8603)
                      (line 39) (byte 1739))
           (launch-r2
               (&spacecraft (*pioneer-spacecraft*))
               (&launch-dest
                   (*solar-system* (type (w7-outer))
                                   (ref (def)))))
           (cd (<=> (*ptrans*))
               (actor (*pioneer-spacecraft*))
               (object (*pioneer-spacecraft*))
               (to (*solar-system* (type (w7-outer))
                                   (ref (def)))))
           (p-1875 pioneer-spacecraft was the first
            spacecraft to venture into the outer
            solar-system %period))
```

Figure 4-7: Requesting an Abstract

4.2. Scanner

The original FRUMP had an initial phrase recognition routine, so that multi-word tokens like "New York" or "Palestine Liberation Organization" could be recognized. MCFRUMP implements the same facility, but because FERRET is designed to read a variety of text sources, including the Dow Jones News Service, it must be capable of reading dates and numbers in many different formats. Also, since FERRET is a retrieval system, the parsed output must contain pointers to the original text. Finally, USENET texts contain a much more "header information" than the simple datelines of a UPI newswire story, and this information is formatted in stylized ways.

FERRET's text scanner deals with these initial issues. The text scanner is composed of two LEX programs. LEX is a generator of lexical analysis programs that compiles regular expression patterns into C code [Lesk & Schmidt 75]. Appendix D contains the actual grammars used by these two programs. Figure 4-8 shows the text from the Pioneer text after it has been scanned.

The first of these programs is the number/date scanner (called SCAN), and performs the following functions:

- Converts newsgroup formatted messages into case-frames for Lisp reading. Each article is made into a separate frame.
- Reads the mail-style header information from the messages and puts each header line into a slot in the output frame.
- Inserts file indexing information into the output. Each message is index by file name, and line number and byte position within the file. Byte position tokens are also generated, giving the start of each paragraph and sentence.
- As a part of conversion to Lisp format, punctuation marks in the original text are converted to Lisp tokens. Colons ":" become %COLON, commas become %COMMA, and so on. Capitalization is indicated by a separate token (%CPT) Thus "StarDate" is represented by the Lisp list (%CPT stardate).
- Numbers are recognized and converted to a single format. FERRET recognizes cardinals, ordinals, and fractions, either in numeric form or with the numbers spelled out in English. See Figure 4-9 for examples.
- Dates and times are recognized and converted to a canonical format. The scanner uses a regular expression grammar to

```
(article
    (file (pioneer.txt))
    (line (1))
    (byte (0))
    (subject (%cpt stardate %colon %cpt march 3 %cpt pioneer 10))
    (from ((special email "dipper@utastro")))
    (organization (%cpt u %period %cpt texas %comma %cpt
                        astronomy %comma %cpt austin %comma %cpt tx))
    (newsgroups (net %period astro))
    (date (%cpt mon %comma 3 %dash %cpt mar %dash 86 02 %colon 00
                %colon 18 %cpt est))
    (lisp-date (time 1986 3 3 2 0 18))
    (text ((p 258) %cpt pioneer (number 10) was the first
            spacecraft to venture into the outer solar system
            %period (p 335) %cpt more %dash %dash coming up %period
            (p 355) (time 1986 3 3 -1 -1 -1) %cpt pioneer (number
            10) (p 376) %cpt on (time 1972 3 3 -1 -1 -1) %cpt nasa
            %apostrophe s %cpt pioneer (number 10) spacecraft was
            launched toward the outer solar system %period (p 484)
            %cpt it was to become the first craft to travel beyond
            the asteroid belt %dash %dash and the first to encounter
            mighty %cpt jupiter %period (p 599) %cpt pioneer (number
            10) is now on its way out of the solar system %period (p
            654) %cpt it is now farther from the sun than any of the
            known planets %dash %dash still sampling the environment
            through which it moves %dash %dash and still
            transmitting data back to %cpt earth %period (p 819)
            %cpt the spacecraft was originally designed for a
            mission lasting (number 21) months %period (p 892) %cpt
            its primary mission was to encounter %cpt jupiter
            %period (p 939) %cpt but the spacecraft has done much
            more %period (p 979) %cpt scientists used %cpt pioneer
            (number 10) data to go beyond the previous picture of
            the solar system %dash %dash that of a central sun
            surrounded by a flat disk of planets %period (p 1129)
            %cpt thanks to %cpt pioneer (number 10) %comma we can
            now envision a huge magnetic bubble containing the
            planets and sun %dash %dash a bubble that may be
            streamlined into a teardrop as the sun at its heart
            moves through the galaxy %period (p 1328) %cpt some
            scientists also think this bubble %quote breathes %quote
            %dash %dash expands and contracts %dash %dash with each
            (number 11) %dash year cycle of activity on the sun
            %period (p 1455) %cpt the outer boundary of
                            . . .
            %close-paren %cpt copyright (number 1985) %comma (number
            1986) %cpt mcdonald %cpt observatory %comma %cpt
            university of %cpt texas at %cpt austin (e -1))))
(end-file)
```

Figure 4-8: Sample Scanned Text

recognize the date and time strings, and these are decoded by the PARSEDATE C Library routine written by Leonard Hamey of Carnegie Mellon University. Dates are interpreted relative to the posting date on the text, so that phrases like "Yesterday we talked about" or "On today's date in 1972" can be given exact meaning.

There is a second lexical analysis program that deals with more specialized types of tokens, the SPECIAL programs. This program recognizes (but does not interpret) these items:

- phone numbers
- social security numbers
- electronic mail addresses
- USENET article identification numbers
- global positions indicated by latitude and longitude
- stellar positions given by right angle and declination
- Universal time specifications

Figure 4-9 shows some examples of the token recognition done by the SPECIAL and SCAN programs.

The main value in recognizing these special cases is that it prevents the parser from wasting time trying to interpret them. The last two items, stellar positions and universal time, are included because the astronomy newsgroup published several IAU Circulars in February and March of 1987 in response to the supernova in the Large Magellanic Cloud. These circulars are full of dense technical notation dealing with the positions of astronomical objects and information about them such as their luminosities and spectral characteristics.

The main advantage of using LEX programs to format the input in this way is speed. The scanner can process 57 kilobytes of highly technical text in 55 seconds, or about 10 kilobaud. The grammar for the scanner is easily changed, and the conversion of the numeric and temporal information to a canonical form simplifies the later analysis by the parser.

```
Today                                    (time 1988 7 16 -1 -1 -1)
March 23, 1959                           (time 1959 3 23 -1 -1 -1)
May 29, 1986 at 3:30pm.                   (time 1986 5 29 15 30 0)
Tuesday                                  (time 1988 7 19 -1 -1 -1)
Next thursday.                           (time 1988 7 21 -1 -1 -1)
Yesterday.                               (time 1988 7 15 -1 -1 -1)
Tomorrow.                                (time 1988 7 17 -1 -1 -1)
12,345,678                                    (number 12345678)
15.42                                         (number 15.42)
three thousand, three hundred and thirty three     (number 3333)
two million, three hundred and nineteen
        thousand, twenty three           (number 2.31902e+06)
12th                                          (ordinal 12)
twelfth                                       (ordinal 12)
twelve hundred                                (number 1200)
the fifty third time                     (the (ordinal 53) time)
the seventh planet                       (the (ordinal 7) planet)
two thirds                                    (fraction 2 3)
Jan 23.45 UT                       (special utime "Jan 23.45 UT")
(800) 123-4567              (special phone "(800) 123-4567")
123-45-6789                     (special soc "123-45-6789")
uucpfoo!miller@uunet.uu.net
             (special email "uucpfoo!miller@uunet.uu.net")
<56@stanton.TCC.COM>(special artid "<56@stanton.TCC.COM>")
Feb. 23.124 UT                  (special utime "Feb. 23.124 UT")
79 56' 48" W 40 26' 33" N
         (special latlon "79 56' 48\" W 40 26' 33\" N")
R.A. 5h35m49s, Decl -69 17'57"
         (special stpos "R.A. 5h35m49s, Decl -69 17'57\"")
```

Figure 4-9: Sample Scanner Output

4.3. The McFRUMP Parser

The core parser is a reimplementation of FRUMP called MCFRUMP. The original FRUMP was written in M-expression Lisp to run on a Dec-10 computer. M-expression Lisp looks a little like Pascal, and is converted by a pre-processor to UCI Lisp. Gerald DeJong was kind enough to provide a copy of the source to FRUMP for use in the FERRET project, but the pre-processor was not available, and the output would have required extensive modification in any event.

It was decided to recode the parser into Franz Lisp, but to keep the lexical and script knowledge.

There are a few important differences between the two parsers:

- MCFRUMP uses a simpler form of the sketchy scripts, which makes the task of learning new script a little easier (the less information in each script, the easier it is to construct a new one).

- MCFRUMP does not implement issue skeletons, which are used in FRUMP to understands collections of scripts (giving FRUMP a recursive flavor). The added complexity would be a burden on the learning component.

- MCFRUMP tries to find all possible meanings of a sentence, rather than just the first feasible meaning. This allows FERRET to assign an ambiguous text to two or more categories. Unfortunately, it means that MCFRUMP runs slower than FRUMP because it deals with many more partially built structures.

- the phrase handling routine is extended to handle some of the special lexical tokens generated by the text scanner; for example, an electronic mail address like (special email "fuzzy@c.cs.cmu.edu") is hooked into the type hierarchy as a *HUMAN-DEF* (specific person).

- MCFRUMP has hooks that allow the dictionary interface to attempt to find meanings for words that are not in MCFRUMP's lexicon.

Figure 4-10 shows the internal structure of MCFRUMP, which is almost identical to that of FRUMP. The components shown are:

- The text scanner that has already been described. It passes its output to

- The phrase handling component. This is an initializing step performed once for each document. Phrases are collapsed into single tokens. These are stored in

- The word array. Each token in the processed text is stored as an element of an array of tokens. This allows a clause to be represented as a pair of numbers (the starting and ending words). The word array is first used by the

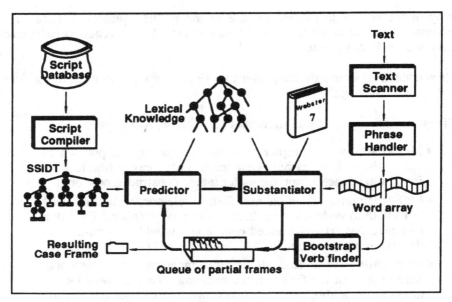

Figure 4-10: The MCFRUMP Parser

- Initial verb search routine, which bootstraps the prediction/substantiation procedure. The word array is searched left-to-right until a structure building word is found. That partial structure is added as the first entry to the

- Queue of partial structures. This list is used by the predictor to perform a breadth first search of the possible concepts representing the input text. The predictor pops the top structure off of the queue and tries to extend it using the substantiator. If the substantiator can extend the structure, the new structure (or structures) is added to the end of the queue.

- The script database contains all of the sketchy scripts used.

- The script compiler takes the scripts and compiles them into a discrimination tree called the

- Sketchy Script Initiator Discrimination Tree (or SSIDT for short). This is the main structure used by the

- Predictor, which makes predictions about what concepts might be found in the Text. These predictions are confirmed by the

- Substantiator, which examines both the partial structure being built and the word array to confirm or disconfirm the prediction.

This component also performs simple anaphora resolution. Whenever a noun phrase is parsed into a conceptual entry, the current context is searched for a previously built concept that are more specific than the current word or phrase, and if found it is substituted. The substantiator uses the

- Lexical knowledge base to determine whether a given word in the word array can have a particular meaning. For example, if the predictor is looking for a person, and the substantiator finds VIRGINIA, there is a match, and the substantiator builds a slot-filler containing a feminine first name, indicating a particular person. If the predictor had been looking for a location, the substantiator would have instead built a structure for the state of Virginia. The lexical knowledge is stored as a collection of FRAMEKIT frames. If the word is not in the lexicon, the

- Dictionary interface tries to find it in *Webster's*. If the word is found, the dictionary interface builds a FRAMEKIT frame and adds it to the lexical knowledge (for this run only).

The major processing path is the loop shown in bold in Figure 4-10. The predictor takes a partial structure off the queue and tries to predict an extension. The substantiator attempts to confirm the prediction, and if so it places the extended structure on the end of the queue. If the predictor finds a complete structure, that structure is emitted as one parse of the input sentence, and the processing continues until either the queue is empty or the pre-determined CPU time limit is reached (this is set at run-time, and was 8 minutes per text, with a maximum of 3 minutes on any one sentence).

4.3.1. The Lexical Knowledge Base

The lexical knowledge base used in MCFRUMP is an expanded version of the knowledge base used in FRUMP. But instead of using Lisp properties and hard-wired code for inheritance, the entire FRUMP database has been reformatted into FRAMEKIT frames [Carbonell & Joseph 85]. There are three kinds of frames that store information about words:

English tokens   For every English word in the knowledge base there is a frame with the same name. These frames list the possible word senses for the given token. For example, the word IMAGE has two senses, IMAGE1 and SEE1. Thus the ambiguity of words is represented at the token level.

Word senses   For each word sense, there is a single frame. Information
                       stored at this level includes part-of-speech. For verbs
                       and adverbs the BUILD attribute stores a partial CD struc-
                       ture and the NEWROLES attribute indicates which case
                       markers are expected to mark the fillers of the CD primi-
                       tive. For example, SEE1 is a verb, and has the following
                       frame:

```
(see1
    (pos verb)
    (newroles
        ((inst) (*detector*) (pobject
    using))
        ((inst) (*detector*) (pobject
    with))
        ((inst) (*detector*) (pobject
    through))
        ((object) (*physobj*) vobject)
        ((actor) (*higher-animate*) subj))
    (build ((<=> (*perceive*)))))
```

So when SEE occurs in the input, and the SEE1 word sense
is selected by the verb finder, the partial structure built is

```
(cd (<=> (*perceive*)))
```

And there is special information to indicate that the actor
is likely to be a higher-animate in the subject position,
the object is likely to be a physical object in the direct
object position, and the instrument, if any, is probably a
DETECTOR in a case marked by "using," "with" or
"through."

For nouns, there is a concept entry pointer. For example,
the word sense IMAGE1 is a noun, and its concept entry is
IMAGE.

Concept entries   This is a conceptual hierarchy or IS-A structure. For
                       example, the entry *IMAGE* is the class of all pictorial
                       representations, and is stored in the type hierarchy as an
                       instance of an *MOBJECT*. Figure 4-12 shows a portion
                       of MCFRUMP's IS-A hierarchy.

The relation between "see," "image" and "photograph" is shown in
Figure 4-11. Note that the verbs SEE1 and PHOTOGRAPH1 are identical except
that the word "photograph" implies that the instrument of the action is a
CAMERA.

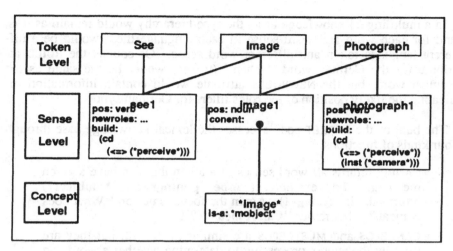

Figure 4-11: Types of Lexical Information in MCFRUMP

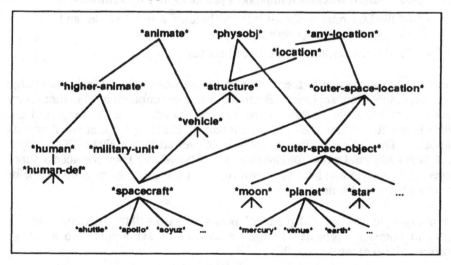

Figure 4-12: Part of the MCFRUMP IS-A Hierarchy

Note that much of the syntax information for the English language is stored under the word sense entries for the verbs in the NEWROLES slot. There is a default role-location list, so for most verbs the NEWROLES list is relatively short. Extra role locating information is given only where there are special constraints on the filler or where unusual case markers are implied by the verb. For example, the instrument of the SEE1 verb sense must be a detector of some kind such as a camera or a telescope.

In a multilingual knowledge base, the type hierarchy would remain as it is, and for each word and word sense in each language there would be a different language token and different word sense. Of course, the BUILD attribute for the German word "sehen" (to see) would be the same as the English word, but the NEWROLES attribute would contain information indicating the likely position of the roles fillers for German syntax.

The bulk of the FERRET code accesses the lexical knowledge base through four kinds of functions:

- CANBE, returns all word senses of a token that can have a given meaning. For example, (canbe 'photograph '*mobject*) returns the list (image1). Again the focus is not on "What does X mean?" but rather "Can X mean Y?"

- CANBEPOS and MUSTBEPOS are similar to CANBE, but they are used by the syntax processing to determine whether a word can be a noun or whether it must be a preposition, for example.

- GET-BUILDS returns the BUILD attribute of a word sense, and is used by the bootstrap verb finder.

- GET-SENSES returns a list of word senses.

For the FERRET system, there are two extensions to the lexical knowledge base representation scheme. Both are used to implement the dictionary lookup. When a call to one of the routines listed above is made, and the word is not found, the *Webster's* dictionary is checked for that word and its variants. The entire dictionary entry is converted into a FRAMEKIT frame, with two additional slots: DEFINITION and SYNONYM. Then the access functions use synonym and near synonym rules to tie the unknown word to one or more known word senses.

For example, the word "picture" is not in MCFRUMP's lexicon, but the entry in *Webster's* returns "image" as one of its synonyms. So a call of (canbe 'picture) works like this:

```
1.(canbe 'picture '*mobject*)
Using synonym of 'picture' => (image1)
(w7-picture-1)
```

```
2. (pf w7-picture-1)
(w7-picture-1
    (pos noun)
    (definition
        (tableau %comma tableau %open-angle stage
         %underscore %close-angle)
        (a transitory visible image or reproduction)
        (image %comma copy %open-angle the
         %underscore of his father %close-angle)
        (a description so vivid or graphic as to
         suggest a mental image or give an accurate
         idea of something)
        (a representation made by painting %comma
         drawing %comma or photography))
    (synonym
        (situation)
        (tableau tableau)
        (movies)
        (motion-picture)
        (image copy)))
```

Thus the system can determine that a "picture" can be a mental object, and that as such it is a synonym of "image." The dictionary interface is discussed in Section 4.4.

4.3.2. The Sketchy Script Database

The second most important knowledge source, after the lexical knowledge, is the script database. In MCFRUMP the scripts themselves are stored in FRAMEKIT frames, and the syntax of the original FRUMP frames was simplified and converted into a FRAMEKIT representational style. The differences are exemplified by the old and new versions of the "vehicle accident" script shown in Figures 4-13 and 4-14.

The old script format is converted at read time into the new format. Note that there is some loss of detail about slot fillers, making MCFRUMP a little less careful (or picky) about its interpretation of events. This simplification is possible because the information retrieval application is not quite as demanding as the translation and summarization done by the original FRUMP.

When the scripts are read in to the Lisp, there are compiled into the discrimination tree (SSIDT). There are really three such trees, one each for actions, state changes, and state indications. A portion of MCFRUMP's *ACTIONS* tree is shown in Figure 4-15.

```
;THIS IS THE NEW FRUMP "VEHICLE ACCIDENT" SCRIPT

[ (CLASS SCRIPT)
  (SVARIABLES &OBJ1 &OBJ2 &LOC &OBJ3 &OBJ4)
  (BUNDLE %CASUALTY )
  (SINITIATORS R1 R0 R2)
  (ACTIVE R1 R2)
  (GEN ABC DEF) ]

[R0 ((<=>($VEHICLE-ACCIDENT ACTOR &OBJ1 OBJECT &OBJ2)) LOC &LOC)

(SINIT ((<=> ACTOR) NIL)
       ((<=> OBJECT) NIL)
       ((LOC) NIL) )

(SVARS (&OBJ1 (<=> ACTOR) *VEHICLE*)
       (&OBJ2 (<=> OBJECT) *PHYSOBJ*)
       (&LOC (LOC) *LOC-DEF*) ) ]

[R1 ((ACTOR &OBJ1 <=> (*PROPEL*) OBJECT &OBJ2) LOC &LOC)

(GEN ABC DEF)

(SINIT ((ACTOR) *VEHICLE*)
       ((OBJECT) *PHYSOBJ*)
       ((LOC) NIL) )

(SVARS (&LOC (LOC) *LOC-DEF*)
       (&OBJ1 (ACTOR) *VEHICLE*)
       (&OBJ2 (OBJECT) *PHYSOBJ*) ) ]

[R2 ((ACTOR &OBJ3 <=> (*PROPEL*) OBJECT &OBJ4) LOC &LOC)

(GEN ABC DEF)

(SINIT ((ACTOR) *VEHICLE*)
       ((OBJECT) *HUMAN*)
       ((LOC) NIL) )

(SVARS (&LOC (LOC) *LOC-DEF*)
       (&OBJ3 (ACTOR) *VEHICLE*)
       (&OBJ4 (OBJECT) *HUMAN*) ) ]
```

Figure 4-13: The Original FRUMP Vehicle Accident Script

```
(script
    (vehac-r1
        (graph
            (cd
                (actor (:req &obj1 *vehicle*))
                (<=> (*propel*))
                (object (:req &obj2 *physobj*))
                (loc (:opt &loc *loc-def*))))
        (init (t))))

(script
    (vehac-r2
        (graph
            (cd
                (actor (:req &obj3 *vehicle*))
                (<=> (*propel*))
                (object (:req &obj4 *human*))
                (loc (:opt &loc *loc-def*))))
        (init (t))))
```

Figure 4-14: The MCFRUMP Vehicle Accident Script

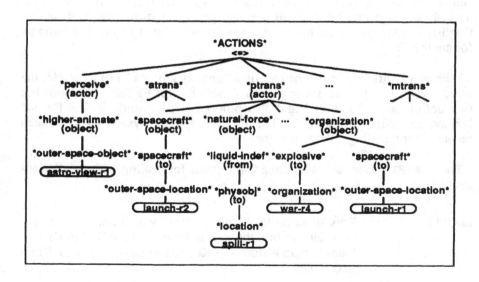

Figure 4-15: A Portion of FERRET's SSIDT

This structure was one of the major contributions of DeJong's thesis, because it allows script selection to be done in logarithmic rather than linear time. Aside from the format changes and simplifications, the SSIDT is the same in both FRUMP and MCFRUMP.

4.4. Dictionary Interface

The use of On-Line dictionaries is currently a "hot" topic in natural language processing, but it is not new. FERRET uses *Webster's Seventh New Collegiate Dictionary* published by G. & C. Merriam and provided in a computer readable form built by James L. Peterson of the University of Texas at Austin [Peterson 82], [Merriam 74]. Several other projects have used the *Webster's Seventh* dictionary, including [Amsler 80], [Amsler 81], [Binot & Jensen 87], [Fagan 87a] and [Jensen & Binot 87]. Another on-line dictionary commonly used is *The Longman Dictionary of Contemporary English*, or LDOCE [Alshawi 87], [Boguraev & Briscoe 87] and [Walker & Amsler 86].

Most of these projects used a more detailed or deep analysis of the on-line dictionary than that provided by the MCFRUMP dictionary interface, but the simpler processing used by MCFRUMP is still quite effective. With no natural language capability at all one can get the part-of-speech of 68,766 English words, synonyms for 58,197 words and related forms and variants for another 25,863.

With just a little analysis, one can find "near synonyms."For example, the word "venture" has no synonyms in common with FRUMP's lexicon, but two definitions ("to offer" and "to proceed") use words in the FRUMP lexicon to define "venture." The original FRUMP system had no such resource for handling unknown verbs.

The FERRET system contains three C programs for dealing with the dictionary:

LOOKUP   This function takes one or more words and uses inflection rules to find the root definition in the *Webster's* file. Sample output from LOOKUP is shown in Figure A-12 on page 165.

DTL   "Dictionary to Lisp" converts the *Webster's* card format into Lisp S-expressions. The synonyms and definitions are separated and stored in different slots in the output frame. Sample output from DTL is shown in Figure 4-16 and also in Figure A-13 on page 166.

DFMT   For debugging and testing, the DFMT or "dictionary formatter" produces human readable versions of the definitions either as an ASCII file or as Scribe^{tm} text formatter commands. Sample typeset output is shown in Figure A-11 on page 164.

When the syntax functions CANBE, CANBEPOS, GET-BUILDS or GET-SENSES cannot find a word in the core lexicon, LOOKUP and DTL are used to generate a frame for the missing word. If the word is in the dictionary and one of the word's synonyms is in the lexicon, the relevant information is retrieved from the synonym.

If the word is found but none of the synonyms are known, the definitions are searched according to these rules:

- for nouns, each head noun in the definition that is not in an example usage is proposed as a possible synonym.
- for verbs, the definition is checked for simple infinitive forms such as "to *verb*" or "to *verb marker*," and if the match is successful, the defining verb is proposed as a synonym.

Using *Webster's* can greatly slow the parser, because there are often several possible definitions proposed for each word found there. Each represents a path through the SSIDT that must be checked by the predictor and substantiator. Most of these paths are invalid, but when a valid one is found the system has understood a sentence that would otherwise have been missed. Without the constraints provided by the scripts in the SSIDT, the simple approach to using the dictionary would be far less successful.

4.5. Case Frame Matching

The sketchy script matcher is responsible for searching the abstract database and retrieving those abstracts that are sufficiently similar to the abstract of the user's query. The current model of the matcher is simple yes/no matching.

copy[1] ('käp-ē) n. [ME *copie*, fr. MF, fr. ML *copia*, fr. L, abundance—more at COPIOUS] 1. an imitation, transcript, or reproduction of an original text, engraving, or photograph 3. *archaic* something to be imitated :: MODEL 4. matter to be set up for printing or photoengraving, syn see REPRODUCTION.

copy[2] vt. 1. to make a copy of 2. to model oneself on —vi. 1. to make a copy 2. to undergo copying.

syn IMITATE, MIMIC, APE, MOCK: COPY implies duplicating an original as nearly as possible; IMITATE suggests following a model or pattern without precluding some variation; MIMIC implies a close copying esp. of voice or mannerisms for sport or for lifelike simulation or representation; APE may suggest presumptuous or servile or inept imitating of a superior original; MOCK adds to MIMIC the clear implication of derisive intent

```
% lookup copy | dtl
(copy (senses w7-copy-1))
(w7-copy-1
    (pos noun)
    (definition (an imitation %comma transcript %comma
                    or reproduction of an original text
                    %comma engraving %comma or photograph)
                (something to be imitated %colon %colon
                    model)
                (matter to be set up for printing or
                    photoengraving))
    (synonym (model) (reproduction))))
(copy (senses w7-copy-2))
(w7-copy-2
    (pos verb)
    (definition (to make a copy of)
                (to model oneself on)
                (to make a copy)
                (to undergo copying))))
```

Figure 4-16: Sample Input and Output of Dictionary Lookup

The Lisp code for the matcher was extracted from the KAFKA frame transformation language [Mauldin 84a] and extended to allow atoms to match if the datum was an instance of the pattern. For example, the Lisp atom *JUPITER* matches *PLANET*, *OUTER-SPACE-OBJECT* and *PHYSOBJ* as well as matching *JUPITER*. Other work on case frame matching, including the scoring of partial matches has been done by Brzustowicz and Carbonell [Brzustowicz 80], [Carbonell & Brzustowicz 84].

Inputs to the script matcher are the parse (or abstract) of the user's query and the list of parsed texts (the abstract database). The output is a list of abstracts matching the user query, including the indexing information necessary to find the original text file, and the post-phrase-processing version of the sentence or sentences that were matched.

Thecurrent matcher is sufficient for testing the performance of the parser for the purposes of this investigation, but would have to be modified for use on larger databases. The current matcher can match a case frame to a pattern, but that implies a linear response time, since the entire abstract database must be searched.

In a production version of the system, the same inverted file technique used to provide fast retrieval response for keyword systems could be applied to case frames, with a logarithmic blow-up of storage required. There are three major parts to this technique:

1. For each atom in each case frame in the abstract database, make an inverted file containing that atom and the index/address of the case frame in which it appears.

2. Expand the basic inverted file from Step 1 by making entries for each super-category of each atom. For N abstracts the average tree height will be $O(\log N)$, so there will be a logarithmic expansion of the storage necessary. In practice, type hierarchies are very shallow, so this expansion may be almost constant.

3. Now when matching a case frame pattern, one need only check the frames given by the intersection of the inverted lists for the elements in the pattern. This will require approximately the same amount of time taken by keyword oriented inverted file methods, multiplied by a constant reflecting the time to evaluating the matching predicate.

Building such a fast matcher would be an important part of any future work on case frame oriented information retrieval. It would be especially useful to reduce the amount of storage expansion necessary. In addition, the current matcher gives a simple binary answer: yes this matches or no it does not. There would almost certainly be value in writing a matcher that gives a *degree of match* score.

4.6. User Interface

For testing purposes, a small user interface has been written that allows the user to enter CD patterns to retrieve texts. The user interface performs the following tasks:

- Prompt the user for a CD pattern
- Format and display the list of retrieved documents
- Allow the user to display any of the retrieved documents in a pop-up window.
- Record which documents the user considers relevant to the query.

This last function is important for the learning component. After the user has marked the texts he considers relevant, a triple consisting of the query, the list of retrieved texts and the list of relevant texts is stored for later use by the learning component to try to find new scripts that give better results for that query than were previously possible.

Although the test version of the interface was command line oriented, it is likely that a graphical or mouse-driven user interface would be preferable. In our envisaged future implementation, after the user had entered a query (parsed by a real natural language query parser), the resulting list of relevant documents could be manipulated by the mouse. The same idea of pop-up windows would be used, but the user would have to expend less effort in the marking process. It is also important that the user be given an "abort" button, so that if for some reason he does not have the time, energy or inclination to give the system feedback, at least he could tell the system that this is so. Otherwise he might simply exit the retrieval system, giving the impression that none of the retrieved documents were relevant. This assumption could bias later learning efforts or cause the system to waste time trying to improve on a script that already works well.

4.7. Summary

So far we have described a complete demonstration of knowledge-based information retrieval, as shown in Figure 4-17. The MCFRUMP parser provides the classification of input texts as instantiated sketchy scripts, and the case frame matcher and toy user interface provide the retrieval and display functions. The *Webster's* dictionary provides an enhanced understanding capability over the original FRUMP program.

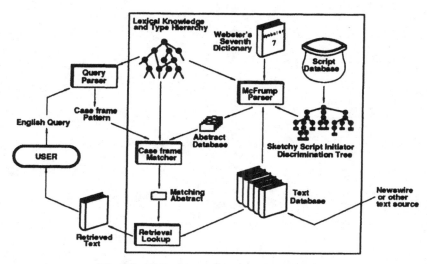

Figure 4-17: FERRET without Learning

Even without a real query parser, this system could be used to scan a stream of text for information relevant to a fixed set of relevance criteria (much like a newspaper clipping service). But as it stands, this system would be difficult to maintain. Language is not a stable medium, but changes constantly as new ideas emerge and are described. Even were that not so, the English language is so vast that we cannot soon hope to write a single computer program to comprehend it all. One way around this complexity is for the system to adapt to its input and to learn from its mistakes. We examine one method for providing a limited kind of learning in the next chapter.

Chapter 5
SCRIPT LEARNING

How index-learning turns no student pale,
yet holds the eel of Science by the tail.
—Alexander Pope
The Dunciad

We have shown how a parser with sufficient world knowledge available to it, in the form of *scripts* can understand, index, and retrieve textual information. The difficulty lies in providing that parser with the necessary abundance of these scripts. In the current work, we show that a variant of the *generate and test* learning method called a *genetic algorithm* can enable the parser to discover new scripts on its own, thus holding out the hope that systems can be built that acquire some of their own world knowledge from the texts they index.

5.1. Approaches to Machine Learning

Our statement of goals from Chapter 1 includes this goal:

> The algorithms used to implement this system must not require unreasonable amount of *maintenance*...

But the FERRET parser is critically dependent on the expectations from its script database to make sense out of the texts it reads. Covering a substantial fraction of the texts in the astronomy domain requires 10 sketchy scripts. FRUMP needed 63 sketchy scripts to cover just 10 percent of the UPI Newswire. These structures represent episodic and situational knowledge, and cannot be gleaned from the *Webster's* dictionary. Clearly, maintaining and extending the script database can represent a major effort, undermining our goal of low maintenance.

Our solution, as suggested in Section 1.6.3, is to use *machine learning* to allow FERRET to expand its own world knowledge. Machine learning is the long sought after "Holy Grail" of computer science. The dream is that if one can build a computer program that can learn *enough*, then programming will no longer be necessary. Our goal is much less ambitious: have the system be flexible enough to deal with holes in its knowledge of a domain by using the knowledge it does have to help fill in the holes.

A good introduction to the general field of machine learning is [Michalski et al. 83]. Other texts such as [Rich 83] and [Winston 84] contain good introductory descriptions of past research in machine learning. Many approaches to machine learning are based on searching through a problem space of possible solutions to find better solutions. While there are many different "camps" of machine learning researchers, two types of approaches are relevant here:

- knowledge independent search (weak methods)
- knowledge intensive search

The weak methods are search techniques that are broadly applicable, but may learn "slowly" and are less powerful. Section 5.2 discusses "genetic learning," which is used by FERRET. Genetic learning is an example of a weak method, and was chosen for this study precisely because it is broadly applicable: it almost always learns *something*.

Examples of knowledge intensive search, or "discovery," include Lenat's AM and EURISKO programs. These learn by "discovering" new concepts that are combinations and modification of concepts they already know [Lenat 79], [Lenat & Brown 83], [Lenat et al. 83]. AM successfully re-discovered much of standard number theory working from first principles and a large set of "discovery" heuristics. AM ran into difficulty as it delved deeper into mathematics because its original learning heuristics were less and less useful. EURISKO was an attempt to solve that problem by learning new heuristics.

For parsers that use scripts to guide the parsing process, learning new concepts means learning new scripts. Gerald DeJong has proposed plan generalization as a mechanism for learning new schemata (which are just like scripts) [Dejong, G. 81], [DeJong, G. 83a]. The method is very knowledge intensive, in that the system must first thoroughly understand one plan before it can generalize to learn a new concept. Raymond Mooney and DeJong implemented these ideas in a text processing system called GENESIS [Mooney & DeJong 85]. The program could answer questions about stories it had read, and could learn new schemas from one story that would help it to understand other stories.

We have already seen in Section 2.3.2 that RESEARCHER learns to understand text better as it reads. RESEARCHER is an example of a program that
learns by applying its knowledge to modify its structures. A very different
form of concept learning was used in Rik Belew's dissertation on the use of
connectionist learning to improve the retrieval performance of an IR system
based on associative networks [Belew 87a], [Belew 87b]. Using feedback
from the user in the form of YES/NO answers to whether a document is
relevant (as in *relevance feedback* in Section 2.1.6), the AIR program adjusts
the weights on links in its network to adapt to the user's ideas about
relevance. The program can also create new nodes and links. This same
kind of feedback is used, albeit differently, in FERRET's learning component
(see Section 5.3.1).

5.2. Tools for Learning: Genetic Algorithms

The theory of evolution, or more specifically *natural selection*, was introduced to explain how animal species changed and adapted themselves to different environments. Early in the history of artificial intelligence, researchers suggested that by simulating this process in software, computer
programs could be made to improve their performance on a given task [Fogel
et al. 66].

One way to formulate the learning problem is to define a language of
possible solutions to a given task, and then design an objective function that
assigns a score to each possible member of the set of possible solutions. By
searching through this space, one learns by finding better and better solutions. Thus the learning problem can be cast as one of *function optimization*,
where a credit assignment algorithm assigns a *payoff* to each point in the
problem space.

Where this mapping is unimodal, standard weak methods like hill climbing
or more powerful algorithms like Newton's Method quickly find the optimal
point in the space. But when this paradigm is applied to more difficult
problems, the payoff functions generally lack properties required for these
methods to work. Almost all interesting machine learning problems map
onto this more complex space.

Holland and DeJong investigated the mathematics of this process, and
demonstrated both empirically and theoretically how crossover and mutation
in an evolving population of sample solutions from a space can be used to
locate maxima and minima within that space [Holland 75], [DeJong, K. 75],
[DeJong, K. 80], [DeJong, K. & Smith, T. 81].

They have shown that genetic algorithms are well suited to domains that do not meet the stringent requirements of standard function optimization techniques (such as differentiability, continuity, or unimodality) [Bethke 81], [DeJong, K. 75], [Holland 75]. Genetic algorithms are heuristic in that they find good but not necessarily optimal solutions. In many applications, such as the travelling salesman problem, finding the optimal solution can be NP-complete [Garey & Johnson 79]. Genetic algorithms are also being used to learn state spaces [Rendell 83], to play games [Smith, S. 80], and to build adaptive user interfaces [Holland 80].

Classically, genetic algorithms solve the black-box function optimization problem: given an effective procedure for analyzing the value of a function at a given point, allocate trials over its domain in an attempt to find the maximum value of the function. Some models concentrate solely on finding the maximum, and others attempt to maximize average performance of a population of candidate solutions. Since function optimization is usually cast as a minimization problem, some transformation is needed to convert minima to maxima for the genetic algorithm.

Genetic algorithms represent points in the function space by bit-strings. For example, if the domain of the function is the set of all real numbers, each number can be represented in fixed-point binary notation, and the corresponding bit-string is merely the concatenation of n binary numbers (Bethke discusses Gray coding as an alternative representation [Bethke 81]). Each bit in the string is called a *gene*, and the values of "0" and "1" for each gene are called *alleles*. A particular bit-string is called a *genotype*. These terms are borrowed from Mendelian Genetics [Holland 75]. It is also possible to use non-binary encodings of candidate solutions, and indeed, FERRET does just that—each member of the population is a CD-graph. In general, though, the more the information is packed into atomic entries, the less effective the mutation and crossover operators become.

Figure 5-1 shows pseudo-code for a *single replacement* genetic algorithm (Holland R_1), that is, an algorithm that replaces a single string at a time. The *EvaluateTrial* routine decodes the chosen representation and evaluates the function at that point. *SelectGood* randomly chooses a string from the gene pool using weighted probabilities such that a string's probability of being selected is proportional to its past performance (*value*). This weighted selection provides the evolutionary pressure that causes the system to improve its trials, or "learn." *SelectReplace* chooses a string to be discarded in favor of a new string to be generated by the genetic operators. Holland discusses discusses the mathematics for replacement algorithms that choose a replace-

```
for i ← 1 to poolsize
  begin
      genepool[i] ← RandomString ();
      value[i] ← EvaluateTrial (genepool[i]);
  end

for t ← 1 to n
  begin
      father ← SelectGood (genepool, value);
      mother ← SelectGood (genepool, value);
      new ← SelectReplace (genepool, value);

      Cross (father, mother, new);
      Mutate (new, prob_mutate);

      value[new] ← EvaluateTrial (genepool[new]);
  end;
```

Figure 5-1: R_1, A Single Replacement Genetic Algorithm

ment uniformly randomly [Holland 75]. For this study, the *SelectReplace* routine always chooses to discard the worst performer. This provides additional evolutionary pressure towards improved performance, and also assures that for a gene pool of size M, the M-1 best strings found so far are always in the gene pool.

Generation of new strings is handled by the *crossover* and *mutation* operators. Crossover chooses a random point between 1 and the string length and concatenates the left half of the father with the right half of the mother (some algorithms discard two strings and keep both offspring from the crossover). The crossover operator is subtle, and results in far better performance than a simple random mutation with preservation of the best [Mauldin 84b].

Crossover is analogous to sexual reproduction in nature, and is useful in search because beneficial features arising in two separate structures can be combined into a single, descendant, thus greatly increasing the odds that such combinations can arise. Figure 5-2 shows two family trees for the same populations with and without crossover (the ancestors are shown at the bottom and the descendants are shown at the top of the figure). Assume that the horizontal and vertical bars indicate favorable, dominant genes (for

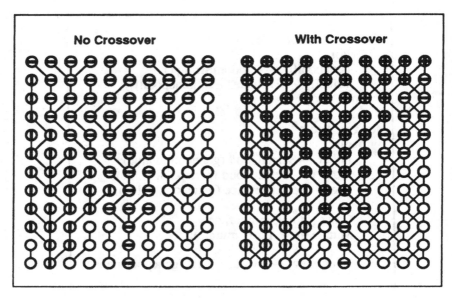

Figure 5-2: Crossover as Sexual Reproduction

example, sharp claws and pointy teeth). Either mutation alone is beneficial but rare, so it is unlikely that in the asexual case (without crossover) that the second mutation will occur a second time in the descendants of the first mutation. With crossover, the first offspring of a sharp clawed parent and a pointy toothed parent will inherit both characteristics.

The mutation operator is primarily used to introduce new alleles into the gene pool. Other operators such as *inversion, dominance change,* and *generalized crossover* have been discussed [DeJong, K. 75], [Holland 75], but these tend to have either a small or adverse effect on problems with only a few thousand trials.

Another class of genetic algorithms is the *generation* model (Holland R_d), where each string in the gene pool is evaluated and then a whole new gene pool is generated from the previous one. This class of function optimizers was studied thoroughly by Ken DeJong [DeJong, K. 75].

5.3. Design of Learning Component

To apply the genetic learning paradigm to the problem of learning scripts for our natural language parser, we need to provide two things:

- A method for generating a new script from one or two old scripts (the analogues to mutation and crossover), and
- An objective function that scores each individual script's performance so that by optimizing this function new and better scripts will be found.

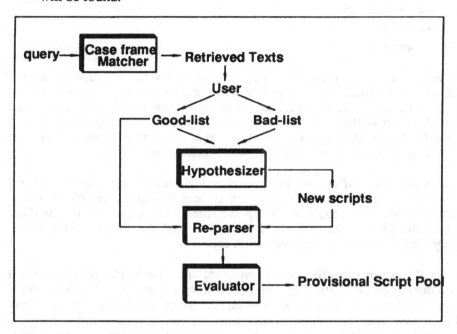

Figure 5-3: Learning Component Architecture

Figure 5-3 shows the block diagram of the learning component that performs both the generation and evaluation of new scripts.

5.3.1. User Feedback

The learning component in FERRET is driven from user feedback obtained during the retrieval process. Once the user has retrieved a set of documents, each document is marked relevant or irrelevant. Thus the set of retrieved documents is divided into a *good list* and a *bad list*. This is the least amount of information we can request from the user. For simplicity, we assume that the user is:

- truthful
- knowledgeable
- consistent
- complete

FERRET depends on the user indicating the relevance of each document. FERRET is incapable of determining that the user is lying (as might be the case if the user were to experiment with the system to see what it might do under certain kinds of uncertainty), or has no understanding of the subject at hand (as could happen in a library if a 5 year old were allowed to play with the ''nice buttons'' while the parent was checking out a book).

In some cases, of course, the user may legitimately not know whether a given text is relevant to the query (it may be a subject outside of his under-standing, or the text could be written in a foreign language). To handle these cases, the user should be given a third choice of *don't know*. This would only slightly complicate the evaluation code.

We also assume that the user is consistent in his feedback. If the same text and query pair are marked as both relevant and irrelevant, the various scores used by generate and test become equal, giving the learner no direction. FERRET assumes consistency across users, as well as for individual users. It would be possible to have individual user models, and thus protect serious users from spurious retrievals produced from frivolous users. But this would also prevent concepts learned from one user to help find texts for another. Thus the twelfth person to query the system about an important current topic (a political story or news about cold fusion, for example) would get a far better answer than he might if each user had to start building a user model from scratch.

Finally, we assume that the user is complete, the user must mark all relevant texts as relevant, not just the few that will suffice to answer the query. This is merely a convenience for the current study, and in a system intended for use by real users, either the *don't know* option would have to be available, or a *punt* button, so that the system would know that the user has not correctly marked each text (perhaps because he does not have sufficient time to wade through all of the retrieved texts). This way the system could avoid attempts to learn from incomplete data.

The end result on the user selection process, called a "data point," is a triple:

- The original natural language version of the query, along with the CD pattern derived from the query, which is used to match each abstract
- A list of "good" abstracts, that represent positive instances of the query
- A list of "bad" abstracts, that represent negative instances of the query

Each abstract is also a four-tuple containing

- A pointer to the disk file containing the original text
- An instantiated sketchy script representing the original text
- A conceptual dependency graph of the concept matched
- The scanned text of the sentence that was parsed (that is, after the lexical processing but before the parsing).

After the texts have been divided into two sets, they are fed to the learning component as shown in Figure 5-3. The first step is to hypothesize new scripts from the *good list*.

5.3.2. Schemes for Hypothesizing New Scripts

The essential feature of any genetic "hypothesis" mechanism is that it rewards better performance by making the attributes of successful structures more likely to occur in the off-spring. The most common mechanism is to select the parent or parents of a new structure using *linearly weighted probabilities* so that the better the performance of the structure, the more likely it is to be chosen as a parent (choosing weights proportional to rank orderings is an alternative method that is less sensitive to the distribution of objective values). For learning sketchy scripts, this coupling is achieved in

FERRET by using the intermediate results results of one query as raw material for the next learning cycle.

When a story is retrieved, either correctly or incorrectly, in response to a user query, it seems likely that the script(s) used to parse that story are closer in conceptual space to the user's query than a randomly chosen script would be. So by chosing such a script or scripts as a parent for the next generation, there is a reward mechanism to drive the system to better scripts.

There are three operators used by FERRET to generate new scripts, once the parents have been chosen:

- generalization (removing restrictions or whole slots)
- specialization (adding restrictions or whole slots)
- crossover (taking slots from one or the other parent)

The first two operators are also used in non-genetic systems (see [Mitchell 77] for example). But in the information retrieval domain, the outcome of a query can guide the selection between these operators. When a retrieval set has a very low precision, specialization is more fruitful, allowing a more precise concept to be found that still matches the relevant documents from the set. Similarly, when the precision is very high, generalization relaxes the constraints on the matcher, and can result in more relevant documents being found the next time a similar query is processed. The third operator, crossover, is the key to the learning algorithm being a genetic one. The full FERRET type hierarchy is shown in Figure A-10, and a subset is shown in Figure 4-12.

Figure 5-4 shows the actual algorithm used to choose a genetic operator. This particular scheme is only one of many possible such schemes, but it does have the following intuitively desirable features:

- When precision is high, the most likely operator is *generalization*. The more general the script, the more texts it will likely retrieve, so recall may be improved by sacrificing some precision.
- When precision is low, the most likely operator becomes *specialization*. More specialized scripts that still match the relevant documents are chosen and improve precision.
- Except when precision is very high, all operators are active at some level of probability.

```
precision ← length (good) / (length (good + bad))

father ← RandomMember (good)
mother ← RandomMember (good)

if father and mother and father <> mother and
   PercentChance (75 - precision) then
   offspring ← Cross (father, mother)
else if (PercentChance (25)) then
   switch Random (1, 4)
      case 1: offspring = Generalize (Generalize (father))
      case 2: offspring = Specialize (Generalize (father))
      case 3: offspring = Generalize (Specialize (father))
      case 4: offspring = Specialize (Specialize (father))
   end
else if (PercentChance (precision)) then
   offspring = Generalize (father)
else
   offspring = Specialize (father)
```

Figure 5-4: New Script Hypothesis Algorithm

5.3.3. Genetic Operations on Case Frames

The genetic operations described in Section 5.2, mutation and crossover, work on bit strings. But the scripts used in FERRET are represented as case frames. How do the operators work with this new representation?

The classic mutation operator is replaced by the two new operators, generalization and specialization. To generalize a case frame, a slot filler is selected at random from the frame, and is replaced by a more general concept from the type hierarchy (by going up the IS-A links). For specialization, a more specific concept is chosen by going down the IS-A links in the hierarchy.[*]

---

[*]In Figure 5-4, there were four more mutation operators: generalize-generalize, specialize-specialize, generalize-specialize, and specialize-generalize. The primary purpose of allowing such double operations was to allow lateral moves in the type hierarchy (by moving up one link and back down). In the studies described in Chapter 6 however, these operators never generated useful scripts.

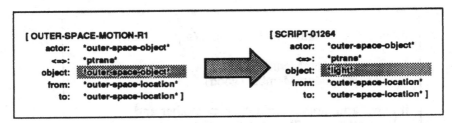

Figure 5-5: Hypothetical Example of Script Specialization

For example, in Figure 5-5, the OUTER-SPACE-MOTION script is changed by specialization into a RADIATE script by specializing the object of the frame (in the FERRET hierarchy, *LIGHT* is an instance of *OUTER-SPACE-OBJECT*).

Crossing two case frames is also a simple matter. Two parent scripts are chosen, and for each type of slot, the filler of the offspring is randomly chosen with equal probability from one of the two parents. If one parent has no value for the slot, the offspring does not have that slot. Thus crossover can generalize, by removing slots, and specialize, by adding slots.

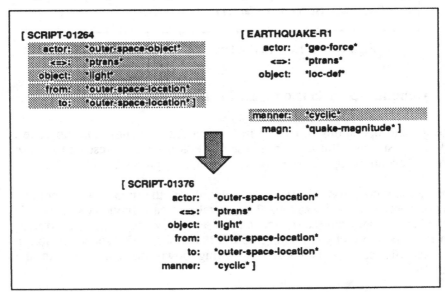

Figure 5-6: Hypothetical Example of Script Crossover

Figure 5-6 shows an example of crossover. The RADIATE script from Figure 5-5 is crossed with the EARTHQUAKE script, resulting in a new "pulsar" script. All but one output slot comes from the first parent, but the MANNER slot is inherited from the second parent. The result is a script for "cyclically emitting light." This script would be useful for parsing descriptions of pulsars and variable stars. In fact, the first user query from Appendix B.2 is a question about stars that "vary in brightness over time." Had FERRET generated this script, it would have performed much better on that particular query.

5.3.4. Is FERRET Really Genetic?

The essence of the genetic algorithm is the *crossover* operator. It allows useful learning results from multiple paths to be combined into a single result. When the objects being learned are case frames, crossover can be achieved by choosing slots from each parent frame to construct a single child.

With such an operator in use, the learning algorithm is definitely *genetic*. On the other hand, because the operators are somewhat more constrained than the purely random operators considered in [Holland 75], it is not at all clear that the mathematical analysis Holland uses to analyze simpler algorithms still applies in this case.

In the learning studies described in Chapter 6, although several provisional scripts were generated by the crossover operator, only one led to a "reasonable" script, and that script did not have any effect on retrieval performance. The greatest single factor in the increased recall performance from the learning component is the *generalization operator*. So in that sense FERRET is not really genetic, but is more properly classed as a generate and test learning algorithm. But the generalization and specialization operators can only change slot fillers, they cannot affect the structure of the script. When a slot must be added or deleted, the crossover operator is the only way to generate that script. For some scripts, the learning component cannot be complete without the chance of crossing two other scripts. Section 7.3.3 discusses the utility of genetic algorithms for learning new scripts.

5.3.5. Evaluation

Once the hypothesizer has generated a pool of new scripts, they must be evaluated. This is done by the *re-parser*. The MCFRUMP parser is run on the retrieved texts using only the new scripts. The query itself is not reparsed. The abstracts from the reparsing are matched against the original query, and new precision and relative recall performance measures are calculated for each script.

Given the data point from the original query, plus the list of good and bad matches, the evaluation proceeds as follows:

1. Start an instance of the MCFRUMP parser
2. Build a new SSIDT using only the newly hypothesized scripts.
3. Reparse each sentence from each abstract (good or bad).
4. Match the original query against each new abstract, calculating for each script how many good texts it matches and how many bad texts it matches.
5. Sort the new scripts by increasing precision and increasing generality. Thus the evaluator prefers scripts that are more precise but also that are less specific (because they are likely to have higher recall as well).

The hypothesis and evaluation process can be repeated over a given data point, but the current version of the learning component only performs one round of genetic learning to propose a "provisional sketchy script." The two best scripts generated are added to MCFRUMP's sketchy script database, and the entire text collection is reparsed (this takes up eight minutes of CPU time for each text).

5.4. Example of New Script Being Learned

Figures 5-7 through 5-9 show an example of a new concept being learned from an old one. This is a real example from the comparison study described in Section 6.4. Figure 5-7 shows one request from the prototypical LAUNCH script. This script assumes that the object being launched is a spaceship. But one of the STARDATE stories about the Hubble Space Telescope contains the following sentence:

```
(launch-r2
    (graph
        (cd (actor (:req &spacecraft *spacecraft*))
            (<=> (*ptrans*))
            (object (:req &spacecraft *spacecraft*))
            (to (:req &launch-dest *outer-space-location*))
            (from (:opt &launch-source *ground-location*))
            (time (:opt &encounter-date *time*))
            (mode (:opt &encounter-mode *mode*)))))
    (init (t)))
```

Figure 5-7: The Original $LAUNCH Script

*In 1986 a telescope will be launched into outer space.**

This sentence is not matched by the original LAUNCH script, because telescopes are not listed as spacecraft in the FERRET conceptual hierarchy (see Figure 5-8).

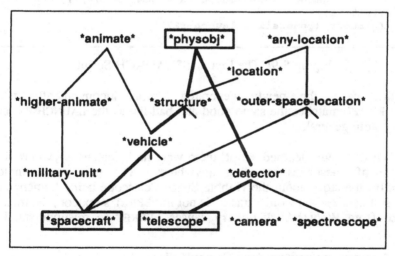

Figure 5-8: Spacecraft *vs* Telescope in the IS-A Hierarchy

If the script learner has a good model of the domain, as might be the case in an explanation based learning system, then it might already know that the

---

*This particular STARDATE script was written before the *Challenger* disaster. The Hubble Space Telescope was eventually orbited on April 25, 1990.

telescope is the object of the launch, and would find the covering concept of
PHYSOBJ by graph theory. Without such a model, however, the system
must fall back on some kind of search. By randomly specializing, generalizing, and crossing scripts (including the LAUNCH script), the hypothesis generator proposes several possible new scripts, and the evaluation module
chooses as best the script shown in Figure 5-9. Since the random steps are
limited to links in the type hierarchy, there is a fair chance that the correct
slot filler will be found in a few dozen steps.

```
(script-r37127
   (graph
      (cd
         (actor (:req &spacecraft *physobj*))
         (<=> (*ptrans*))
         (object (:req &spacecraft *physobj*))
         (to (:req &launch-dest *outer-space-location*))
         (from (:opt &launch-source *ground-location*))
         (time (:opt &encounter-date *time*))
         (mode (:opt &encounter-mode *mode*))))
   (init (t))
   (history (generalize launch-r2)))
```

Figure 5-9: The Learned $LAUNCH Script

In this case, the newly generated script, inconveniently named
SCRIPT-R37127, matches the same good and bad list as the LAUNCH-R2 script,
but it is more general.

Without the newly learned script, there were no instances anywhere in the
database of telescopes traveling anywhere. The new script matches
(correctly) the story about the Hubble Space Telescope being launched into
orbit. But because the word "track" is not in FERRET's lexicon, the meaning
gleaned from *Webster's* dictionary causes FERRET to misunderstand the
sentence

   Telescopes are now tracking Comet Halley.

to mean that "Telescopes are traveling to Comet halley." The only way to
fix the second match is to fix the lexicon. We cannot exclude the meaning
simply by changing the script expectations, because telescopes can (and
have) been sent to probe planets and comets.

```
Ferret, 11-May-89, from Franz Lisp, Opus 38

1.load-db telescope
[load-db /usr/mlm/src/txt/ferret/database/telescope.abs]
telescope
2.ferret
                  Top level interface to Ferret

Show sentences [y/n]: y
Do learning    [y/n]: n

Enter CD pattern: (cd (<=> (*ptrans*))
                         (object (*telescope*)))
[ Found 2 articles ]

Articles matching (cd (<=> (*ptrans*))
                          (object (*telescope*)))

   1] StarDate: March 2  Space Telescope
      ((In 1986 a telescope will be launched into outer
        space)
       (This telescope is due to be launched by the
        space-shuttle in mid 1986))
   2] StarDate: August 22  Comet Halley Before Dawn
      ((Large telescopes are now tracking comet-halley))

Choice (or 'q' to quit): a 1
Abstract: ((reference (file f500/star.8503)
                      (line 1) (byte 0))
            (no-script)
            (cd (<=> (*ptrans*))
                (actor (*shuttle1* (ref (def))))
                (object (*telescope* (ref (def)))))
            (p-1021 %cpt this telescope is due to be launched
             by the space-shuttle in mid %dash number-1986
             %period)
            (script-r37127
                (&spacecraft (*telescope* (ref (indef))))
                (&launch-dest (*space*)))
            (cd (<=> (*ptrans*))
                (actor *physobj*)
                (object (*telescope* (ref (indef))))
                (to (*space*)))
            (p-140 %cpt in number-1986 a telescope will be
             launched into outer space %period))
```

Figure 5-10: Retrieval using newly learned Launch script

5.5. Caveat

The use of generate and test for learning by discovery was studied by Lenat in his AM and EURISKO programs. Although initial work was extremely promising, Lenat has subsequently warned that the methods used were specific to the mathematics domain [Lenat & Brown 83].

The learning component used in FERRET is very similar in some respects to that used in AM, so there is concern that the same limitations apply. But there are three reasons that FERRET is not necessarily subject to these limitations:

First, since FERRET uses conceptual dependency as its knowledge representation, the syntactic operations used by the script hypothesizer are closely related to semantic modifications in the underlying conceptual space.

Secondly, FERRET is guided by feedback from the user about which concepts are worthwhile; it does not rely totally on predetermined heuristics. This direction from the user can prevent the learning component from going too far astray in searching for new concepts.

Thirdly, FERRET's learning component is intended to fill in holes in the domain description generated by humans, not to discover unaided whole areas of conceptual meaning. In the given example, it simply did not occur to the original programmer that a spacecraft launch would involve objects other than spacecraft. By patching one of the existing scripts, FERRET was able to overcome that omission and still retrieve the document.

5.6. Summary

Just as the role of the dictionary interface described in Chapter 4 is to amplify the human effort of creating the lexicon, the role of the learning component in FERRET is to amplify the work of the human in creating a collection of sketchy scripts to cover a given domain.

Figure 5-11 shows a block diagram of the FERRET system with the learning component in place. Feedback from the user and trace information from the MCFRUMP parser guide the learning component in generating new scripts that are added to the script database. These new scripts then allow the parser to find more meanings in the text database on subsequent reparsing.

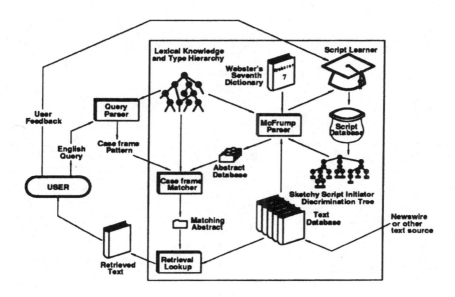

Figure 5-11: FERRET plus Learning

Chapter 6
EMPIRICAL STUDIES

If your experiment needs statistics, you
ought to have done a better experiment.
—Ernest Rutherford

This chapter describes our experiments to determine the retrieval effectiveness of FERRET and its various components. The key study was the comparison of FERRET's recall and precision performance versus boolean keyword search. That study is described in Section 6.4.

6.1. Domains for Studying Retrieval

This section discusses the various domains to which FERRET has been applied. For reasons described in Section 6.1.3, the STARDATE texts were chosen as the major focus of this study.

6.1.1. UseNet

The FERRET system was specifically designed for reading and classifying USENET news texts. Because extensive world knowledge is necessary for the parser to read multiple categories of texts, this study did not include results from a large cross section of the USENET news system. Instead, the astronomy newsgroup was chosen as a focus for this study. There are four kinds of text that appear regularly on SCI.ASTRO:

STARDATE   Until March of 1987, the University of Texas McDonald
                  Observatory published the daily transcripts of the NPR
                  STARDATE radio program on SCI.ASTRO.

IAU Circulars   In February of 1987, a supernova was discovered in the
                       Lesser Magellanic Cloud. This was an extremely rare
                       event that caused a great deal of traffic in SCI.ASTRO.
                       Fifty announcements from the (IAU) were cross-posted
                       in SCI.ASTRO. These texts are extremely technical and
                       full of astronomical jargon.

WantAds   A significant portion of the articles are posted by in-
                       dividuals buying and selling equipment or asking for
                       advice about buying equipment.

General Discussion By far the bulk of the SCI.ASTRO traffic are discussions of
                       individual questions about astronomy and astrophysics.
                       These texts are sometimes difficult to index because they
                       rely heavily on discourse and no single article (except for
                       the original question) can be understood by itself.

6.1.2. Dow Jones News Service

After the FERRET system was running, Carnegie Mellon obtained access to
the Dow Jones news service. Although no comprehensive studies were done
of FERRET's performance on the Dow Jones texts, a format converter was
written that reads the Dow Jones format and converts it to a form that looks
like a USENET article. This simple format change, plus a few new scripts,
allowed FERRET to read portions of the Dow Jones news wire.

```
Article 0007 of 9999, Mar 13 06:35.
Subject: BRITISH TELECOM 3RD QTR NET PROFIT 306 MILLION POUNDS
Newsgroups: dow.jones
Date: 13-Mar-87 06:35:00 EST
Service: dj

  British telecommunications PLC pre-tax profits rose to 506
million pounds in its third quarter ended Dec. 31 from 452
million pounds a year earlier.

  8:11 Am
```

Figure 6-1: Sample Dow Jones News Story

For example, Figure 6-1 shows an excerpt from a Dow Jones newswire
story. The augmented text scanner converts phrases like ''506 million'' to
single lisp tokens like (**number 5.06e+08**) to simplify the parsing process.
The scanner also handles date and time specifications like ''Dec. 31.''

```
(rise (senses rise1 rise2))

(rose (senses (rise1 ppart) (rise2 ppart)))

(rise1
    (pos verb)
    (newroles
        ((from) (*measure*) (pobject from))
        ((to) (*measure*) (pobject to))
        ((actor) (*measure*) subj))
    (build ((toward (*number* value (*higher*)))))))

(rise2
    (pos verb)
    (newroles
        ((from) (*direction*) (pobject in))
        (((actor) (object)) (*outer-space-object*) subj))
    (build ((<=> (*ptrans*) to (*sky*)))))
```

Figure 6-2: FERRET's definitions for "rise"

Figure 6-2 shows the definitions for "rise" and "rose." Stock market reports use the word "rise" to describe changes in measures such as profit, cost, and average. One simple script, INDICATOR-CHANGE, suffices to cover almost half of the Dow Jones newswire, because the bulk of the traffic concerns changes in prices or other stock market activity. Figure 6-3 shows how this story is parsed.

But since FERRET devotes a large fraction of its domain description to astronomy, the word rise also describes the motion of the sun, moon, planets and stars in the heavens. Figure 6-4 is a one sentence excerpt from a longer text about the moon rising. Figure 6-5 shows how the parser can choose the correct meaning of "rise" based on the attributes of the other elements in the sentence.

6.1.3. The StarDate Database

In 1986 the decision was made to focus on the STARDATE scripts, and a collection was started at CMU. Since the radio program is aimed at a general audience, the texts are written in simple English and the subject matter is interesting but not demanding.

```
McFrump,   6-Sep-88, from Franz Lisp, Opus 38

1.run-mcfrump profrise.scn

Working on article (reference (file profrise.txt)
                              (line 1) (byte 0))
Sentence: (p-163 bty-co %cpt plc pre-tax profits rose to
          number-506000000.0 pounds in its ordinal-3
          quarter ended time-december-31-1987 from
          number-452000000.0 pounds a year earlier
          %period)

******* rose (rise1) builds:
  (cd (toward (*number* (value (*higher*)))))
Parse Rule 2 fills 'actor' with
  (*profit* (type (pre-tax1))
            (quantity (*plural*)))
Parse Rule 2 fills 'from' with
  (*pound* (quantity (452000000.0))
           (per (*year*)))
Parse Rule 2 fills 'to' with
  (*pound* (quantity (506000000.0)))

******* rose (rise2) builds:
  (cd (<=> (*ptrans*)) (to (*sky*)))
Parse Rule 2 fills 'actor' with (*bty-co*)

Accepting script
  (ind-change-r1
      (&indicator
          (*profit*
              (type (pre-tax1))
              (quantity (*plural*))))
      (&direction (*number* (value (*higher*))))
      (&new-value (*pound* (quantity (506000000.0))))
      (&old-value
          (*pound* (quantity (452000000.0))
                   (per (*year*))))
      (&time
          (*date* (month december)
                  (day 31) (year 1987)))))
Parsing time: 122.06
```

Figure 6-3: Parsing the Sample Dow Jones Story

```
Article 980 of 7 Oct 87.
Subject: StarDate: October 7  Jupiter and the Moon
From: dipper@utastro
Newsgroups: sci.astro
Date: 7-Oct-87 02:00:00 EST

Wednesday night the moon rises in the east in evening twilight.

Script by Deborah Byrd.
```

Figure 6-4: Astronomy story using ''rise''

```
McFrump,   6-Sep-88, from Franz Lisp, Opus 38

1.run-mcfrump moonrise.scn

Working on article (reference (file moonrise.txt)
                              (line 1) (byte 0))
Sentence: (p-148 time-october-7-1987 night the-moon rises
              in the east in evening twilight %period)

******* rises (rise1) builds:
   (cd (toward (*number* (value (*higher*)))))

******* rises (rise2) builds:
   (cd (<=> (*ptrans*)) (to (*sky*)))
Parse Rule 2 fills 'actor' with (*earths-moon*)
Parse Rule 1 fills 'object' with (*earths-moon*)
Parse Rule 2 fills 'from' with (*east*)

Accepting script
 (astro-view-r2
     (&view-object (*earths-moon*))
     (&view-loc (*east*))
     (&view-date (*date* (month october) (day 7)
                          (year 1987))))
Parsing time: 63.11
```

Figure 6-5: Parsing the Astronomy Story

Since the texts are meant to be read aloud over the radio, they are highly narrative. That is, the information is conveyed sequentially without reference to charts, graphs, figures or references to other articles in the newsgroup. This matches most closely with the way natural language programs like FRUMP read text: one word at a time.

An initial collection of 279 articles was collected from SCI.ASTRO NETNEWS postings, and used to design and test the early versions of the MCFRUMP parser. The percentages of texts understood shown in Table 6-6 were calculated using 98 of these texts.

For more complete evaluation, a larger collection of STARDATE transcripts was obtained directly from the McDonald Observatory. This larger set consisted of 1065 texts representing three years of radio broadcasts from January 1, 1985 to December 31, 1987, and included all of the texts in the initial collection of 279 described above.

These were sorted intro chronological order and numbered from 1 to 1065. The collection was split into a training set and an evaluation set (odd numbered texts were used to test and train the learning code, and even numbered texts were stored away unexamined until the final evaluation was performed). So there are four different collections of texts used throughout the empirical studies:

- the original set, with 279 texts
- the whole set, with 1065 texts
- the training set, with 533 odd numbered texts from the whole set
- the evaluation set, with 532 even numbered texts from the whole set

6.1.4. The Astronomy Domain Description

FERRET started with the script database and lexicon from FRUMP. Since this database was oriented towards the UPI newswire, there was very little conceptual overlap with the content of the SCI.ASTRO newsgroup. To handle astronomy, a domain description consisting of a script database and lexicon was written with 5 basic scripts (using 10 requests in all). This database took one graduate student about 40 hours to write. The basic scripts are:

LAUNCH	sending a space probe to outer space
ASTRO-POS	an astronomical body being in a particular relationship with another
OUTER-SPACE-MOTION	
	an astronomical body moving in a given relationship to another body
SPACETRAVEL	people traveling to or from an astronomical body
ASTRO-VIEW	an astronomical body being viewed by or visible to someone

To support these five scripts, the lexicon from Frump was extended with additional frames for objects and actions that occur commonly in astronomy texts. There are:

- 965 frames for
- 442 words representing
- 251 concepts using
- 272 words senses.

Common extensions included words for seeing things (image, photograph, glimpse), for certain kinds of motion (orbit, launch, rise), plus a great many proper names (of stars, comets, planets, nebulae, and constellations). The content of the lexicon was adjusted by running the parser several times on the initial set of 279 STARDATE radio texts. The scripts and lexicon were fixed, however, before the larger dataset was obtained from McDonald Observatory.

6.2. Parsing Effectiveness

After a domain description was written, the parser was run on a set of the first 98 texts from the initial set of 279 (that is the first 98 texts sorted by date). The script database included the 63 scripts used by the original FRUMP to parse UPI newswire stories, in addition to the 10 astronomy scripts.

The result was that slightly more than 60 percent of all texts were understood "correctly." In this case, that means that either one of the astronomy scripts was chosen as representative of the text (and that the conceptual meaning built thereby was not a misunderstanding), or that the CD graph built was good enough to retrieve the text.

Parsing Effectiveness			
	Understood	Misunder-stood	Total
Found script	57	19	76
Partial Parse	3	19	22
Total	60	38	98

Figure 6-6: Parsing Effectiveness

6.3. Effect of Using Dictionary

To determine how much of this performance was attributable to the diction-ary interface, a comparison study was done by parsing a sample set both with and without time limits.

6.3.1. With Time Constraints

The normal processing mode for MCFRUMP includes a time limit of 8 minutes per text and 3 minutes per single sentence. Because the parser attempts to resolve all possible meanings of a sentence, a highly ambiguous sentence, or a sentence with many pronouns, can require hours to parse. These limits keep MCFRUMP from getting stuck on any one sentence or article.

Early tests of the parser were done on the training set with tighter limits of 4 minutes per story and 2 minutes per sentence. As a control, the parser was run without the dictionary interface using these same limits. The results are shown in Table 6-7. To our surprise, the parser understood more sentences *without* using the dictionary.

Closer investigation of parser traces showed that using the dictionary dras-tically increased the amount of ambiguity resolution required by the parser. Since more words now had plausible meanings, more work was required to confirm or disconfirm possible interpretations of any one sentence.

With the dictionary, sentences appearing earlier in the text were more likely to be parsed, but the parser ran out of time before it read very far into the

Effect of Dictionary, With 4 minute time limit per text			
Number of texts: 533	With W7	Without W7	Change
Total sentences	3312	7492	126%
Misses	2704	5981	
Sentences with some parse	608	1511	149%
Percent "understood"	22.5%	25.3	2.8%
Sentences with script	449	1194	
(percent of sentences read)	14%	16%	2.3%
Sentences with partial parse	159	317	
Size of abstracts (chars)	408k	820k	101%
CPU hours to parse texts	56.6	43.3	

Figure 6-7: Effect of Dictionary with time limits

text. Without the dictionary, early sentences were less likely to be parsed correctly, but there were slightly fewer misunderstood sentences, and the parser often found simpler sentences later in the text that it could understand.

The net result was that more sentences were understood with slightly higher precision without the dictionary. But in some cases, these sentences appeared much later in the text and sometimes dealt with secondary topics.

6.3.2. Without Time Constraints

A second comparison study was performed, this time without any time limits on the parser. This way, the effect of the dictionary on understanding could be studied in isolation from time effects. Because of the increased time needed, a smaller sample of 50 texts was randomly chosen from the training set and used for this study. The results are shown in Table 6-8. This time, the parser understood more sentences with the dictionary than without.

Investigation of parser traces from the second study showed that, like the first test, early sentences were more likely to be understood by using the dictionary, and that the abstracts produced were somewhat more representative of the texts (approximately one fifth of the texts had much more accurate abstracts because the early sentences were better understood).

Effect of Dictionary, With no time limit			
Number of texts: 50	With W7	Without W7	Change
Total sentences Misses	986 704	986 784	
Sentences with some parse Percent "understood"	282 28.6%	203 20.6%	+38.9 +8%
Sentences with script (percent of sentences read)	168 17.0%	147 14.9%	+14.3 +2.1
Sentences with partial	114	56	+103.6
Size of abstracts (chars) CPU hours to parse	151k 43.5	109k 9.7	+40.0%

Figure 6-8: Effect of Dictionary without time limits

6.4. FERRET versus Boolean Keyword Query

To determine the effectiveness of script based text skimming for information retrieval, a comparison study was performed between the FERRET
system and a simple boolean keyword based retrieval system. This is the
most important experiment done, because it relates directly to objective four
given in Section 1.6.4—improve recall and precision.

The user queries were not obtained until after the parser had been run on
the training set of texts and the lexical knowledge base was fixed. This
assured that no changes were made to the system that were specific to queries
used for this study.

6.4.1. Sample User Queries for Studies

The study as planned was to use a set of 50 astronomical queries from the
readership of the SCI.ASTRO newsgroup. These readers were familiar with
astronomy, but had never seen FERRET before. A set of 47 sample queries
was obtained, and these were parsed by the FERRET system to produce a
collection of script patterns for matching against the text database.

Unfortunately, because the request for queries posted to the newsgroup was very non-directive, only 5 of the queries submitted had any overlap with the training database of STARDATE texts. In many cases, FERRET would properly parse the question and produce a good script pattern, only to find that there were no matching articles in the database. So with this first set, the most common result was that neither the boolean keyword system nor FERRET found any relevant articles.

To solve this problem, a new survey form was designed. Each form contained three paragraphs selected at random from the complete database. Responders were instructed to chose one or more paragraphs and give questions that would be answered in part or in whole by retrieving the given paragraph.* In this way it was guaranteed that each user query would have a least one relevant story in the database. The survey was distributed to a list of graduate students in the CMU computer science department in their first to fourth years of study. Twenty-two (22) students submitted forty-four (44) sample queries (the complete list of queries is in Appendix B.2).

6.4.2. The Comparison Retrieval System

For comparison, a STAIRS-like boolean keyword program was used. The test program implemented boolean AND, OR, NOT and adjacency, as well as prefix matching and token matching. The system used was written by the author as two C programs: one to invert a file of text, and one to perform the retrieval operations on the inverted word lists. The following grammar describes the syntax of a retrieval expression:

---

*Much like the *Jeopardy* TV game show: here are the answers, give us the questions.

$$
\begin{aligned}
\textit{expr} \quad &\Rightarrow \textit{expr} \text{ OR } \textit{factor} \\
&\Rightarrow \textit{factor} \\
\\
\textit{factor} \quad &\Rightarrow \textit{factor} \text{ AND } \textit{term} \\
&\Rightarrow \textit{factor} \text{ NOT } \textit{term} \\
&\Rightarrow \textit{factor} \text{ ADJ } \textit{term} \\
&\Rightarrow \textit{term} \\
\\
\textit{term} \quad &\Rightarrow (\textit{ expr }) \\
&\Rightarrow \textit{token\$} \\
&\Rightarrow \textit{token}
\end{aligned}
$$

A custom-coded system was used to insure that line and word numberings would be identical to those given by the FERRET system. It should also be noted that although the keyword system implemented the adjacency operator, none of the queries actually used it (even though the library catalog at CMU uses STAIRS and does have the adjacency operator in it).

The user survey forms requested that each English query be given an equivalent keyword query. In all forty-four queries, the simple keyword system was sufficient to implement the query.

6.4.3. Query Parsing

Since there is no real query parsing component in FERRET, a post processor was used to allow the MCFRUMP parser to act as a query parser.

First, each of the forty-four user queries was parsed by FERRET into a sketchy script pattern. Exactly half (22) of the queries produced some kind of pattern. The other twenty-two queries contained words or concepts that were unknown to the parser. For these queries, the production retrieval system would fall back to using keywords. The important point is that FERRET knows that it does not understand the query, and does not try to apply itself outside of its area of expertise.

The CD graphs produced by parsing the queries were filtered by a deterministic Lisp program to convert them into case frame patterns. The following operations were performed:

Query:

How do I find the constellation Gemini?

Resulting Instantiated Script

```
(astro-view-r1
   (&viewer (*me*))
   (&view-object (*const-gemini* (ref (def)))))
```

Resulting Conceptual Dependency Graph

```
(cd
   (<=> (*perceive*))
   (actor (*me*))
   (object (*const-gemini* (ref (def)))))
```

Resulting Query Pattern

```
(cd (<=> (*perceive*)) (object (*const-gemini*)))
```

Figure 6-9: Faking a query parser with MCFRUMP

- keep only these slots: TO, FROM, OBJECT, ACTOR and <=>
- keep only the head item from each slot filler
- convert all occurrences of *YOU* and *ME* to NIL.

Although the combination of MCFRUMP and post-processor works well in some cases, the lack of detailed syntactic knowledge prevents some reasonable queries from being parsed. In some cases, the raw user queries were rephrased to be more easily parsed. In these cases, both the original and paraphrased queries are shown in Appendix B.2.

6.4.4. Comparison Results

Figures 6-10 and 6-12 show the results of comparing the basic FERRET system with keywords. Each diagram shows 22 vectors and a vector sum. The first figure, Figure 6-10 shows the results of applying the 22 parseable

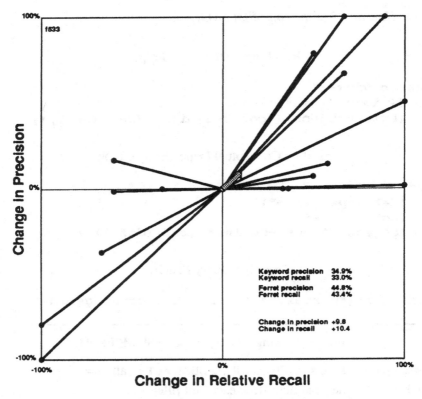

Figure 6-10: Ferret versus Keywords - Training Set

Comparison Results			
	Keywords	FERRET	Change
Precision	34.9%	44.8%	+9.8%
Relative Recall	33.0%	43.4%	+10.4%

Figure 6-11: Retrieval Performance without Learning - Training Set

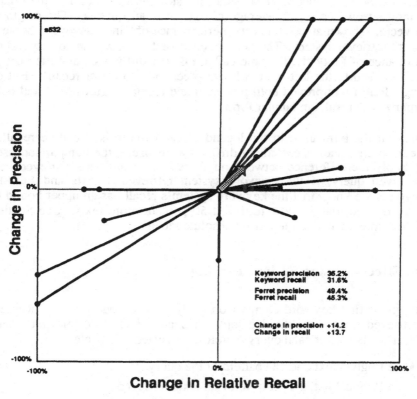

Figure 6-12: Ferret versus Keywords - Evaluation Set

Comparison Results			
	Keywords	FERRET	Change
Precision	35.2%	49.4%	+14.2%
Relative Recall	31.6%	45.3%	+13.7%

Figure 6-13: Retrieval Performance without Learning - Evaluation Set

user queries to the training database of 533 STARDATE texts. Each vector represents the difference in recall and precision performance for one query. The large arrow shows the average change over all queries. The origin of each vector (shown at <0,0>) is the performance obtained using the boolean keyword retrieval system. The head of each vector shows the corresponding performance of FERRET. In some cases, FERRET did worse, and the vectors point done and to the left (that is lower precision and lower recall). But on average, FERRET improved both precision and recall. Figures 6-11 and 6-13 summarize the results in tabular form.

Note that the term used in the legend of each figure is "relative recall." Since absolute recall is extremely difficult to measure, the comparison used was simply the difference between numbers of relevant texts retrieved. So for a given query, if the keyword system retrieved 4 texts and FERRET retrieved 6, we know that the keyword system's recall has an upper bound of 67 percent, and that FERRET retrieved 50 percent more texts. See Section 6.4.7 for more details on measuring absolute recall.

6.4.5. Effect of Using Script Learning

During the first keyword comparison study, as each query was processed, the retrieved texts were divided into "relevant" and "not relevant" sets. The user feedback for each query therefore consisted of a triple:

- the English text and CD pattern of the query
- the "good" list, the set of relevant texts retrieved
- the "bad" list, the set of irrelevant texts retrieved

Each triple is called a "datapoint." These datapoints were saved and used as input to the learning component for the second comparison study: how well the learning component could learn new scripts.

One round of learning (that is, one round of hypothesis and one of evaluation) was run on each query. The gene pool size was set at 25, and the best two sketchy scripts for each query were kept. This gave 44 new scripts.

The parser was re-run with only these 44 scripts over the corresponding text database. This process was repeated for both the training and evaluation set. That is, the learning code was run from the output of the training set, and was used to parse the training set a second time, and the output from the evaluation set was run through the learner and the resulting scripts were used to parse the evaluation set.

The precision and recall performance of the parser with the learned scripts was determined in the same way as the non-learning parser, and the results are shown in Figures 6-14 and 6-16, and summarized in tabular form in Figures 6-15 and 6-17.

These diagrams are similar to the vector diagrams given for the non-learning parser, but each query now is shown as a pair of vectors. The first vector, with its origin at <0,0>, is the difference in recall and precision performance between keyword retrieval and FERRET without learning. The second vector, with its origin at the head of the vector, shows the difference in performance between non-learning and learning parsers. Again, the average over all queries is shown as two large arrows.

The first result to note is that learning greatly improves recall, but slightly reduces precision. This is an intuitive result, because it would be unlikely that an automated learning process could generate "better" scripts than those written by the author of the parser system. Thus each learned script is a poorer representation of the concept than the original scripts provided by the author, so the precision of the matching algorithm should be reduced by learning. On the other hand, the most successful scripts in the genetic learning round were generalizations of the ASTRO-VIEW and LAUNCH scripts, and these generalizations matched many more texts, greatly increasing the recall performance (increasing relative recall from 45% to 80%).

Figure 6-18 shows two of the learned scripts, each of which is a generalization of an original script. The first example, a generalized launch script, allows the retrieval of the sentence

In 1986 a telescope will be launched into outer space.

as described on page 102.

The second example shown is a generalized outer-space motion script, which allows parsing of such sentences as

The object moving towards Venus.

It rises about 4 a m.

Many bodies have eclipses.

Normally this sentence could not be parsed, because "object" by itself is not an outer-space object. But for queries about objects moving toward Venus, there must be some way to parse this sentence for the text to be retrieved.

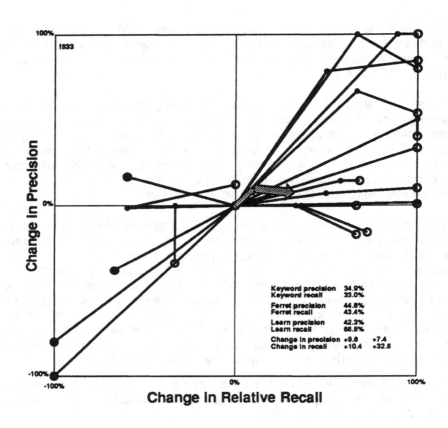

Figure 6-14: Effect of Script Learning - Training Set

Learning Results				
	Keywords	FERRET	Learning	Learning Change	Cumul. Change
Precision	34.9%	44.8%	42.3%	-2.5%	+7.4%
Relative Recall	33.0%	43.4%	65.5%	+22.1%	+32.5%

Figure 6-15: Retrieval Performance with Learning

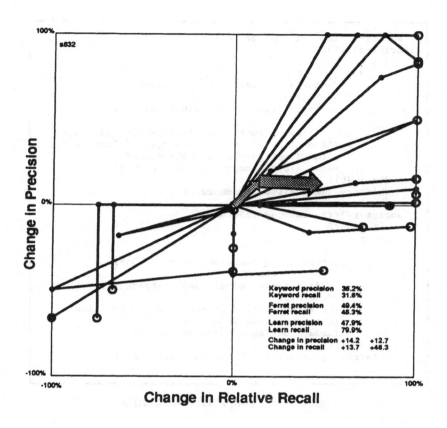

Figure 6-16: Effect of Script Learning - Evaluation Set

Learning Results				
	Keywords	FERRET	Learning	Learning Change	Cumul. Change
Precision	35.2%	49.4%	47.9%	-1.5%	+12.7%
Relative Recall	31.6%	45.3%	79.9%	+34.6%	+48.3%

Figure 6-17: Retrieval Performance with Learning

```
;  script-r37127, matched 58 texts
(script-r37127
    (graph
        (cd
            (actor (:req &spacecraft *physobj*))
            (<=> (*ptrans*))
            (object (:req &spacecraft *physobj*))
            (to
                (:req &launch-dest *outer-space-location*))
            (from (:opt &launch-source *ground-location*))
            (time (:opt &encounter-date *time*))
            (mode (:opt &encounter-mode *mode*)))))
    (init (t))
    (history (generalize launch-r2)))

;  script-r69645, matched 153 texts
(script-r69645
    (graph
        (cd
            (actor (:req &move-object *physobj*))
            (<=> (*ptrans*))
            (object (:req &move-object *physobj*))
            (from nil)
            (to (:req &move-dest *outer-space-location*))
            (time (:opt &move-date *time*))
            (mode (:opt &move-mode *mode*)))))
    (init (t))
    (history (generalize outer-space-motion-r2)))
```

Figure 6-18: Sample Learned Scripts

6.4.6. Speed of Learning

In discussing typical genetic algorithms, it is customary to determine how many iterations are required for the gene pool to converge to an optimal solution. Since there was only one iteration done for this study, and since the most common operator used was generalization (rather than crossover), it is impossible to determine whether the new scripts generated by the learning component would converge, and how long that would take.

In our opinion, however, the learning component as presently constituted would learn very slowly, perhaps too slowly to be of much use. While it is true that one round of generalization greatly improves recall, further generalization would be unproductive, as it would generate the "match everything" script. The learning component would then have to search for minor modifications to the scripts using the crossover operator, and that would yield much slower convergence toward better scripts.

The slow learning is a result of the bottleneck of user feedback with only 1 bit of information for each text/query combination. If a document is never retrieved, it does not participate in the learning process. Suggestions for improved learning algorithms are given in Section 7.3.3.

6.4.7. Absolute Recall

Note that although the recall rating for FERRET with learning as shown in Table 6-17 is almost 80%, remember that this is "relative" recall. So that 80% is only relative to the best performance in each case. The learning version of FERRET often had the best performance of the three algorithms studied, so in those cases it had a relative recall of 100%. That accounts for the high value. The 80% figure is an upper bound, and is only useful for comparison to the values of 32% for keywords and 45% for FERRET without learning.

To determine the absolute recall performance, a sample of 5 of the queries was chosen at random to ensure they would be typical of the larger set of queries. An exhaustive manual search of the evaluation database was performed using these 5 queries, and the results are shown in Figure 6-19. The raw data are given in Appendix C.

Recall by Exhaustive Manual Search			
	Keywords	FERRET	Learning
Precision	31.6%[1]	58.7%[2]	65.2%
Abs. Recall	19.4%	20.0%	52.4%

Figure 6-19: Absolute Recall and Precision for Five Queries

Notes:

1. In 3 of 5 cases, the keyword search failed to retrieve any documents, and was given a precision score of 0 for those cases.

2. In 1 of 5 cases, the basic FERRET system failed to retrieve any documents, and was given a precision score of 0 for that case. This explains why the precision is lower for FERRET without learning than the system with learning.

The results are in basic agreement with the larger comparison study. The keyword recall performance is about 20%, about the same as the original Blair and Maron study discussed in Chapter 1. The precision is only 31.6% instead of the 79% reported by Blair and Maron, but that is explained by the three cases where the precision was not measurable because no documents were retrieved. Most importantly, FERRET with learning retrieved 2.7 times as many documents as keywords (compared to 2.5 times for the entire set of queries). This agreement between the two ratios makes it likely that the large increase in recall is a real increase in performance.

6.5. Possible Sources of Error

In any study where the subjective judgment of the experimenter must be used, there is possibility of bias. This section describes the steps taken in this study to minimize experimenter bias.

6.5.1. In User Queries

The major results of this study were obtained by evaluating sample user queries of the astronomy database. If these queries are not somehow representative of the queries a real system would have to handle, then the performance results may not be applicable to the real retrieval problem. This section describes the steps that were taken to minimize bias in the set of sample queries.

User query survey forms were sent by electronic mail to 123 computer graduate science graduate students. Of these, 22 returned the forms, each with two queries for a total of 44. None of the 22 respondents were professional astronomers or librarians. A sample survey form is given in Appendix B.1.

No sample queries were given to the survey participants. Instead, they were shown real paragraphs from the database chosen uniformly randomly. The random number function used was the UCB RANDOM call from Berkeley Unix.

6.5.2. From Queries to Case Frame Patterns

Given the lack of a real query parser, there was some experimenter participation in the conversion of queries to case frame patterns. This was limited to providing paraphrases for some queries that FERRET could represent, but was unable to parse exactly as given by the respondent. In some cases, a precise representation was unparseable, but a more general concept was given instead. The complete list of user queries and paraphrases used is given in Appendix B.2. Six queries required no paraphrase at all, and 14 required paraphrases. Two queries were parsed, but the parses were wildly wrong (but the incorrect parses were kept and used in the study, and the results counted against FERRET's recall and precision performance).

6.5.3. In Analyzing the Relevance of Retrieved Texts

The most likely source of error in this study is the determination of whether a retrieved text is relevant or not. The bulk of this determination was made by the author, both for measuring keyword performance and FERRET's performance. As a consistency check, the retrieval scores for all three systems (keywords plus FERRET with and without learning) were examined to assure that a retrieved text scored as relevant for one system was given the same score when retrieved by the other systems, ensuring that there was no relative bias in favor of one particular system, although there could be an absolute bias affecting all three retrieval scores equally.

6.5.4. Effects of Time-Constrained Parsing

The improvements due to learning shown in Figures 6-14 and 6-16 may be somewhat overstated due to the effect of time-constrained parsing. Because the bulk of the learned scripts were generalizations, and because the more general scripts were easier to parse in some cases, the parser was able to read farther into some texts using the learned scripts. This would have the effect of increasing recall.

There is no way to reverse engineer the magnitude of this effect. One way to eliminate it would be to re-run the parsing portions of the study with no time limit in effect. This would be prohibitively expensive given the state of the MCFRUMP code and our current computing resources.

In any case, the recall and precision performance shown is real; the only question is how much better the FERRET system could perform if given more time, versus how much better the system performs with learning. Several of the retrieved texts matched, such as the "space telescope" story, could only be retrieved by adjusting the script database, as the learning component did in this study, so the script learning definitely contributed positively to the system's performance.

Chapter 7
CONCLUSION

Even faded ink is better than the clearest memory.
—ancient Chinese proverb

7.1. Objectives Met

Recall from Section 1.6 the goal of this project:

> The goal of the FERRET project is to build and demonstrate a full text information storage and retrieval system called FERRET that uses case frames to provide a conceptual representation of texts and to show that this retrieval system provides better recall and precision performance than is possible with a boolean keyword retrieval system. The algorithms used to implement this system must not require unreasonable amount of maintenance, and must be capable of providing fast response time.

This major goal was divided into four specific objectives. This section revisits these objectives and discusses how our research has met these objectives and what contributions we have made.

7.1.1. Objective 1: Demonstrate conceptual matching on real texts

> The most basic objective of this project is to demonstrate a complete information storage and retrieval system working on real texts that uses conceptual matching as the basis of its retrieval mechanism.

FERRET represents a successful next step in the continuum of knowledge-based retrieval. D. A. E. Lewis demonstrated that case frame similarity is a good measure of "aboutness," but failed to demonstrate how to match the frames themselves automatically [Lewis, D. A. E. 84]. D. D. Lewis showed how to match frames automatically to produce an information retrieval system, but failed to generate the frames automatically from the texts [Lewis, D. D., Croft & Bhandaru 89]. DeJong demonstrated a parser with sufficient robustness to handle real texts, but did not incorporate it into an information retrieval system [DeJong, G. 79a].

Building on these results, FERRET parses the texts into case frames, stores the frames built and retrieves them by automatically matching against query patterns from the end-user. The conclusion of D. A. E. Lewis that case frames can lead to improved retrieval performance (both recall and precision) is also confirmed.

FERRET is a synthesis of these earlier systems, but it also incorporates new elements, including an interface to *Webster's* dictionary that expands the system's lexicon with minimal human effort, a frame matcher (based on the KAFKA system [Mauldin 84a]), and a script learning component.

7.1.2. Objective 2: Use an on-line dictionary to augment lexical knowledge

The goal of low maintenance implies that, where possible, no more human effort should be involved in storing texts than is necessary. To improve the parser's coverage without undue human effort in building massive lexicons, the FERRET system is able to tap information already available in computer form, specifically the *Webster's Seventh Dictionary*.

When confronted with an unknown word, FERRET can find the definition, if any, in the on-line copy of *Webster's Seventh Dictionary*, and can use the part-of-speech, variant forms listings, synonyms and definitions given to relate the unknown word to words already in MCFRUMP lexicon. Using these related meanings, FERRET can often find the correct meaning of the sentence even if the unknown word has multiple meanings listed in *Webster's*. The dictionary access component was described in Section 4.4 and its effectiveness was discussed in Section 6.3.

7.1.3. Objective 3: Use genetic learning to augment script knowledge

The goal of low maintenance also implies that, where possible, the system must be able to learn concepts within its domain with minimal human effort involved. It should not be necessary for the knowledge base implementors to forsee every possible concept that the retrieval system will ever have to match.

The learning component was described in Chapter 5 and its effectiveness was discussed in Section 6.4.5. Using a genetic algorithm, the learning component generated new modifications of pre-existing scripts that significantly improved FERRET's recall performance, at the expense of a slight drop in precision. But unfortunately, the learning contribution came solely from the generalization operator, and not from crossover. Thus the performance increase cannot be attributed to the genetic algorithm itself.

Even though the learning ability represented by FERRET's genetic learning component is rudimentary, it did produce scripts that allowed the retrieval of stories not understood by the basic system. This result is a first step towards systems that improve their own retrieval performance without undue human effort to expand the system's world knowledge. And significant as this first step may be, one can envision future systems with much greater *depth* of understanding, *flexibility* in matching, and greater *adaptability* in handling new texts.

7.1.4. Objective 4: Provide better recall and precision than keyword systems

The ultimate objective of this work is to demonstrate that conceptual understanding provides better retrieval performance; ideally resulting in a substantial increase in both recall and precision performance.

As discussed in Section 6.4, on a database of 1065 astronomy texts, using 44 sample users queries, and with the learning component enabled, FERRET improved precision performance from 35.2 percent to 47.9 percent, and recall more than doubled (relative recall went from 31.6 percent to 79.9 percent). These are respectable improvements: far beyond the gains achievable by merely modifying a boolean keyword search system.

7.2. Applications

Given a robust knowledge-based parser and an effective knowledge representation scheme, many text processing applications beside information retrieval become practical, including text filtering, sorting and routing, and text summarization.

7.2.1. Basic Retrieval

The current FERRET system is designed to be used as an interactive textual retrieval system, in which the user enters a query and immediately receives a list of relevant documents as a response. The options at that point include displaying the text of the retrieved document on the user's terminal.

The same code could be used to implement a library card catalog system, a kind of bibliographic retrieval, where the texts searched are bibliographic entries about some larger collection of text. In this application, the FERRET system would have less of an advantage over boolean keyword retrieval systems, because the fields used in a library catalog system (such as AUTHOR, TITLE and DATE) provide a simple semantic representation of the document. But FERRET's ability to understand the content of sentences may still provide an important capability.

In either of these applications, the conceptual matching provided by FERRET would be used as one option only; the ability to perform a free text search would have to be retained. In the study described in Chapter 6, the prototype query parser could only understand half of the queries. Even assuming a smarter parser, some concepts will simply not be representable by the FERRET system, or will not have been learned or added to the script database. In these cases, a weaker but universally applicable searching technique must be available.

For some queries, too, merely checking for the presence or absence of a given text string is very effective. Proper names are a class of retrievals for which understanding the concepts may not help a great deal. For example, immediately after the nuclear reactor explosion at Chernobyl in 1986, if one wanted to retrieve stories about nuclear reactor accidents in the Soviet Union, simply looking for the keyword "Chernobyl" in the text worked very well. Even so, such a search would have missed highly formal phrases like:

Russian nuclear power plant accidents in the Ukraine

or

Dangers of Large Graphite Reactors

As time passed after the accident, more and more articles began to mention Chernobyl in describing the effects on other countries. In May of 1986, the *Wall Street Journal* and the *New York Times* both mentioned Chernobyl in their reports of a Summit meeting wholly unrelated to the issue of nuclear power. Eventually, the word "Chernobyl" became a popular metaphor for disasters in general and nuclear disasters in particular. By June of 1988, the *Wall Street Journal* used the phrase "post-Chernobyl sentiment" is describing Switzerland's debate over their own nuclear power plants. After a few years, the word "Chernobyl" had lost its specificity.

Another retrieval application would be browsing systems such as the COALSORT system [Monarch & Carbonell 86], or Smith's hierarchical database [Smith, P. 87]. A browsing system is a form of hypertext where documents have a variety of links to other documents. These can be hierarchical (such as INSTANCE-OF, PART-OF or CITES), or unrestricted. In such a database the user starts from a given node or document and "navigates" through the links to find other related documents. The difficulty in creating such a database is linking the documents together, but this is precisely where the FERRET system could be of use. Using the abstracts built by the MCFRUMP parser, various kinds of semantic links could be built automatically (such as SAME-ACTOR-AS, SAME-OBJECT-AS or SPECIALIZATION-OF). The COALSORT database in particular is built on the same kinds of case frames that the MCFRUMP parser is designed to produce.

7.2.2. Filtering

A slightly easier text classification problem is filtering a stream of texts and selecting only those matching some prespecified criteria. Clipping services and digests were around before computers, and today many information retrieval systems allow users to specify a set of keyword patterns that are matched against all new documents. Those that match are forwarded to the user on a regular basis. The INFORMATION LENS system [Malone et al. 87] is just one example of an information system that could benefit from the kinds of natural language processing provided by FERRET.

Another type of filtering technique is provided by Carnegie Mellon's *Andrew Message System* (AMS) [Borenstein et al. 88]. AMS allows users to share classifications of message via "magazines." Any user can decide to "edit" a message area. The editor creates the message area (called a "bboard") within a topic area, and forwards all relevant and interesting messages from other bulletin boards to the magazine. Since there are over 1700 bulletin boards on AMS, the magazines provide a way to see most of the really interesting messages without having to look at every single group. The magazines are arranged under these high level categories:

- current events in china
- games
- computer hardware
- humor (the most popular category)
- hypertext systems
- mail systems
- sports (hockey)
- trivia

Editing a magazine is in some ways a simpler problem than the full storage and retrieval task. The parser need only have enough world knowledge to recognize and understand texts matching its selection criteria. So for simple filtering tasks, the current FERRET system is already sufficient. For example, even with its current world knowledge, FERRET could edit an astronomy magazine. All messages from the whole newsfeed (including USENET and Dow Jones news) could be scanned for astronomical messages.

Other possible applications include the NEWSPEEK and NEWSPRINT systems developed at M.I.T.'s Media Lab [Brand 87]. NEWSPRINT "watches" television by decoding the closed captioning broadcast with the TV signal and capturing selected video images. The NEWSPEEK system combines stories from Dow Jones News Retrieval, NEXIS, XPRESS, wire services and television news. Both are meant to be user-customizable, to give individualized answer to the question "What interesting things happened today?" either in the news or on television. Using its superior understanding capability, the FERRET system could give an even better answer to these questions.

One difficulty is that FERRET is designed to identify *relevant* texts, not necessarily *interesting* ones. Rich's GRUNDY system could recommend interesting books to users based on models built from interaction with the user [Rich 79]. GRUNDY depended on a large knowledge base of book topics that was built by hand. One possible application would be to take document descriptions from FERRET and do the interest matching with a GRUNDY-like system.

In *The Fountains of Paradise* [Clarke 79], Arthur Clarke describes the information retrieval system of the future as having a "Personal Interest Profile." He points out that almost everyone would place their own name at the top of their list, and that some pranksters might also include in their profiles such improbable events as:

- Eggs, Dinosaur, hatching of
- Circle, squaring of
- Atlantis, re-emergence of
- Christ, Second Coming of
- Loch Ness monster, capture of
- World, end of.

With due respect to Arthur Clarke, undoubtedly these events should be included in a global list of events that the entire populace would want to know about immediately.

7.2.3. Sorting and Routing

Unlike the filtering task, which calls for limited coverage, or the retrieval task, where there may be a free text search capability to fall back on, the task of routing texts to various recipients requires complete coverage: every message must go somewhere.

In practice, of course, even the best systems (machine or human) have an other or "miscellaneous" category, so FERRET could direct any non-understandable messages to a human backup. But very good coverage would be needed to make such missed messages the exception rather than the rule.

For example, the Dow Jones News Service assigns symbolic codes to each story that moves on its 90 day news service. Some are company codes such as IBM for International Business Machines or BTY for British Telecommunications Company. Other codes include GOV for government, CPR for computer hardware, PET for petroleum, or SUP for supreme court. Thus a story like:

The Supreme Court overturned the appellate court's ruling on the

government's anti-trust case against IBM. The appellate court had

enjoined IBM from providing computers for British Telecom.

would probably be assigned at least the following codes:

BTY, CPR, GOV, IBM, SUP

These codes are often but not always assigned when the story is written, but some stories are obtained from other newswires and are missing the codes. And even when they have already been assigned, they are checked by hand. The task is handled by a few people whose job is to read each story, determine which codes and company symbols apply to the main parts of the story, and delete any codes that were assigned because of minor or unimportant references. This is a demanding task, because both speed and accuracy are important: the operators only have 90 seconds from the time the story comes in until it must be indexed and sent out on the wire. If the right codes are not assigned, the customers waiting to buy and sell large amounts of stock might miss an important story.

The RUBRIC and TCS systems described in Section 2.3.2 perform exactly this task. By assigning each input text to one or more fixed categories, they allow a stream of undifferentiated messages to be directed to the proper recipient by determining the content of the text.

FERRET's ability to understand the main point of a text, ignore secondary material, and its lexical ability to recognize proper names (including company names) make it capable of doing this job. But the speed and coverage issues would have to be thoroughly addressed before it could be trusted completely. The advantage of the machine is the speed and consistency possible. Since more than one manual indexer is required to keep up with the traffic flow, and since the job goes on 24 hours a day, the same story coming into Dow Jones might be assigned different codes depending on which operator handles the story. Using FERRET, even as a pre-processor alone, might improve both accuracy and consistency.

7.2.4. Summarization

The original FRUMP system provided a multi-language headline service. By extracting only the gist of the text, and leaving the detail, the FRUMP system made the text retrieval task much easier. By providing summaries in other languages, it allowed foreign speakers to identify those texts they would like to have translated into their native tongues.

Finding just the right text from a sea of documents can solve many retrieval problems, but sometimes the user is still overloaded by "interesting, relevant" responses. Within the USENET news system, for example, there is a huge amount of redundancy. One person may post a very interesting question about the advantages and disadvantages of a particular software package. In response, hundreds of people may post their own opinions about the package, both pro and con. Order is restored only after the original poster (or some other kindly soul) collects, digests, and republishes a summary of the answers. But in some cases, no one takes on the summarization task. And occasionally more than one person will post a summary (and who decides who summarizes the summaries?).

The summarization task entails collecting relevant data, discarding redundancy and coalescing the rest into a small package of useful information. This task is made simpler by having a semantic representation of the text, and is impossible without understanding. The knowledge representation ability of FERRET is a first step. But the FERRET parser simplifies the text too much to allow useful paraphrasing of the text. The summarization could be done, but the conversion back into natural language might be impossible without information lost by the FERRET parser. Because MCFRUMP represents meaning only at a coarse level of detail, some facets of meaning are ignored that, while unimportant for retrieval, are crucial for generation of English text from the structure. Once a parser was built that could provide the extra detail, with a similar level of coverage, it could be used not only for language translation and summarization, but also for retrieval.

7.3. Future Work

Before FERRET can be put into practical, commercial use, at least two hurdles have to be overcome: the lack of a query parser, and the slow speed of the current parsing system. Research into better learning algorithms for acquiring new scripts and other domain knowledge would also be very helpful.

7.3.1. User Query Parser

> Answers are the easy part,
> Questions raise the doubt.
> —Jimmy Buffet
> *Off to see the Lizard*

For simple filtering applications, where the selection criteria are relatively constant, the current FERRET system would work. A so-called knowledge engineer would create the case frame patterns from a user specification, and the FERRET system would select all articles matching those patterns.

But in a dynamic, interactive environment, users must be able to specify their own patterns in a simple manner. Natural language queries take advantage of the years the user has spent learning his own language, if and only if the parser is not so brittle that the user cannot predict which phrases will and will not be understood. Thus, a query parser must be broader than a text skimming parser: it must reasonably handle any query the user puts forth. When parsing texts for later retrieval, if the system fails to understand one sentence, the parser may well find another later that allows the document to be retrieved. The text in an article being indexed is larger and more redundant than a simple query. In this sense, query parsing is harder than text parsing.

On the other hand, when a query parser gets confused, finds an unknown word or phrase, or is confronted with an ambiguity, the user is right there, available for clarifying dialog about the query. In the text retrieval task, the author is not readily available for clarification — he may even be dead. So in this sense, the query parsing task is easier than the retrieval task. The result is that query processing is fundamentally different from retrieval parsing, and therefore should be performed by a different parser.

Query parsing has been an area of active research for some time, and there are many impressive systems that can handle retrieval tasks from non-textual databases [Hendrix et al. 76], [Wilensky & Arens 80], [Carbonell et al. 83a]. While this may not be an entirely solved problem, there are query parsers that can do this job today.

Figures 7-1 and 7-2 were taken from [Carbonell et al. 83b]. Figure 7-1 shows sample user queries about computer peripherals being answered by the system in English. In this system the DYPAR-II parser was used to process the user input [Carbonell & Hayes 81]. The DYPAR-II parser combines pattern matching, global transformations, semantic grammar specification, and recursive case-frame instantiation. Figure 7-2 shows a sample user query. and its corresponding output case frame.

When XCALIBUR encounters an ambiguous query, it presents the user with a list of the possible interpretations and asks which is the correct choice. This is the simplest workable resolution strategy. In other cases, the query is not ambiguous but incomplete. In these cases a sub-dialog is started to fill in the necessary slots in the case frame. Then the original query is completed and can be processed.

>*What is the largest 11780 fixed disk under $40,000?*
  The rp07-aa is a 516 MB fixed pack disk that costs
  38000 dollars.
>*Add two rp07-aa disks to my order.*
  Line item 1 added: (2 rp07-aa)
>*Add a printer with graphics capability*
  fixed or changeable font?
>*fixed font*
  lines per minute?
>*make it at least 200, upper/lowercase.*
  Ok. Line item 2 added: (1 lxy11-sy)
>*Tell me about the lxy11*
  The lxy11 is a 240 l/m line printer with plotting capabilities.

Figure 7-1: Sample dialog from XCALIBUR

>*What is the price of the 2 largest dual port fixed
  media disks?*

                    The parser returns:

```
[QUERY
     (OBJECT
          (SELECT
               (disk
                    (ports (VALUE (2)))
                    (disk-pack-type
                         (VALUE (fixed)))
               (OPERATION
                    (SORT (TYPE (*descending))
                         (ATTR (size))
                         (NUMBER (2)))
               (PROJECT (price)) )
          (INFO-SOURCE (*default)) ]
```

Figure 7-2: Parsing a query into a case frame in XCALIBUR

Given that other query parsers have been written that can generate case
frames as output, it should be straightforward to build such a parser for the
FERRET system. But it is a large project. The parser must use the FERRET

knowledge base (with or without the *Webster's* dictionary interface) so that it can generate case frames that are compatible with the output from the skimming parser. It is also possible that the knowledge base for the skimming parser will have to be enhanced, extended, or modified to support the query parser.

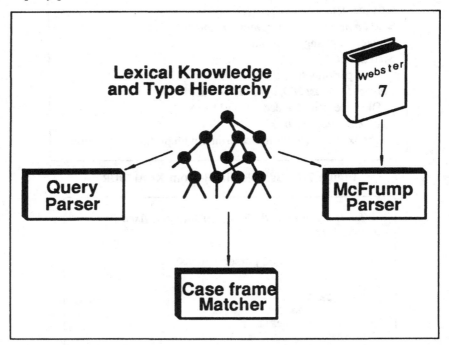

Figure 7-3: Centrality of the Lexical Knowledge Base

The key to a successful retrieval system is that the query parser, the skimming parser, and the case frame matcher all work from the lexical knowledge base (see Figure 7-3). This helps to assure a consistent representation of ideas that allows the matcher to work properly.

7.3.2. Parser Execution Speedup

Two kinds of speed problems must be addressed before the FERRET system can be widely used: the time required to parse the texts, and the time required to respond to a user query.

The MCFRUMP parser used for this study parsed 1,988 kilobytes of STARDATE text in 229 hours on a Microvax II. That's about 2.47 characters per second or 25 baud. The daily traffic on Dow Jones is about 1 megabyte in 8 hours, so a bank of 15 Microvaxes could keep pace with the Dow Jones newswire, with a maximum latency of 8 minutes (assuming that the time budget is set at 8 minutes per text).

There is reason to believe that the current mixture of compiled and interpreted Lisp in the current FERRET system could be recoded to provide a 10 to 100 speedup. Previous experience with the KAFKA system showed similar speedups when the author's style of Franz Lisp was recoded by an experienced Lisp hacker.

The other problem is giving the end-user quick response time. The abstract matching code used for the study in Chapter 6 was a simple linear search through the list of all abstracts, keeping those that matched the frame pattern. For the 1000 abstracts from the STARDATE database, a simple retrieval would take about 20 seconds. Clearly this is insufficient for databases with hundreds of thousands or millions of texts.

As described in Section 4.5, the solution is to replace a fundamentally linear algorithm with one that runs independently of the database size. Keyword systems typically use inverted files (see Section 2.1.2). To use the same algorithm for abstracts, one could try the following:

1. Create an inverted file of all tokens that occur in the abstract database.
2. Given a case frame pattern, treat the tokens in the pattern as a large conjunction.

This fails when a token in the text is an instance of the pattern token. For example, if the pattern is "trips to planets," and the text is "trip to Jupiter," somehow "Jupiter" must be located. One solution is to take advantage of the "bushiness" of hierarchies in lexical knowledge bases. For example, the MCFRUMP hierarchy has a maximum depth of 10 (see Figure A-10 on page 162). So by trading space for time, we can modify the previous algorithm as follows:

1. For each token in the abstract, and for each superordinate concept for that token, add to the wordlist.

Thus the token "Jupiter" would be added to the word lists for JUPITER, PLANET, OUTER-SPACE-OBJECT, OUTER-SPACE-LOCATION, ANY-LOCATION,

LOC-ROOT, PHYSOBJ, PHY-ROOT. Now when the same match is sought, the occurrence of the word "Jupiter" is on the token list for "planet," and the standard list intersection finds the document (assuming the other parts match).

Doubtless there are many important considerations to writing a fast case frame matcher for retrieval, but this technique demonstrates one effective way to trade an $O(N \log N)$ memory requirement for speed within a constant factor of current keyword system performance.

7.3.3. Better Learning Algorithms

As discussed in Section 5.3.4, even though the genetic learning component now used in FERRET does greatly improve the recall performance of the retrieval system, the increased recall comes mainly from generalizing existing scripts, and not from the generation of new scripts by the crossover operator. Were the current algorithm run for more iterations, requiring more CPU time than we had for this study, the generalization operator would fail to produce new scripts, and any additional learning would have to come from crosses between scripts already in the database.[*]

Although we remain convinced that the genetic algorithm used can and would generate useful new scripts for parsing, given that only one reasonable new script was generated in the learning runs described in Chapter 6, it is our opinion that the genetic algorithm as presently implemented in FERRET would learn only very slowly. Since new items must be very much like old items, the rate of concept acquisition may well be too low to keep the system current with the literature in even a slowly advancing field. Clearly a better learning technique must be developed for automatic acquisition of concepts feasible for the parser's knowledge base.

The reason that the current genetic learning component learns slowly is that it relies on random steps to generate new concepts, rather than having a principled mechanism that exploits the world knowledge in the system. It is true that the random steps are constrained to motions within the type hierarchy, and this does improve the hit rate of the hypothesis generator. But these steps are only weakly directed based on the precision of the current user query.

---

[*]Or from the double step operators such as SPECIALIZE-GENERALIZE AND GENERALIZE-SPECIALIZE described in Section 5.3.3.

If a more complete theory of the world is available, then a technique called "explanation based learning" can be used (for a thorough discussion of explanation based learning, see [AI Journal 90]). By exploring the reason a particular solution to a problem works, the learning component can focus its exploration in more productive areas of a problem space. If a future FERRET learning component can ask itself why a particular document was relevant to a user's query (or even ask the user directly), then perhaps it can acquire new domain concepts far faster than the current genetic learning component.

The Latent Semantic Indexing technique, described in Section 2.1.5 may be relevant here. The technique uses Singular Valued Decomposition (closely related to factor analysis) to represent a collection of documents and words by a high dimensional space (between 100 and 200 orthogonal basis vectors). Since the basic operation is still just counting words, the analysis can be applied to texts from any domain with no reliance on large knowledge bases. But with this technique, although closely related words and documents are likely to be close in the reduced space, the meaning underlying the words is not explicit as it is in a parse produced with a hand-built script.

It is an interesting open question whether the LSI technique can be used to handle unknown words by using the LSI metric to find near-synonyms, replacing or augmenting the use of the on-line dictionary described in Section 4.4. Most likely, a hybrid strategy would be best, enabling a real parsing system to fall back gracefully on statistics when working outside of the limits of its world knowledge.

The pessimistic approach to knowledge base acquisition is being pursued by Lenat et al. in the CYC project. CYC is "an attempt to build a single intelligent agent whose knowledge base contains the *tens of millions* of facts...that define our consensus reality" [Lenat & Guha 88], emphasis added. Rather than wait for a breakthrough in learning capability, CYC is using the "Chinese horde" approach, having many hands trained in a single philosophy adding the millions of necessary facts that will make up the system. The big question is whether those tens of millions of facts will be useful to the variety of AI systems by which they are meant to be used. An immediate open question is whether a FERRET-like retrieval system can use the CYC knowledge base to understand text.

7.3.4. Extending the Range of Application

The FERRET parser is best at indexing paragraph-sized chunks of text. But more and more databases are storing whole books and encyclopedias. One possible approach is to index larger texts paragraph by paragraph. In a different context, Robert Amsler has suggested that paragraphs are a more normal unit of text than sentences, and they have the added advantage of being easily identified lexically (just look for blank lines).*

Another possible difficulty is very narrow domains. For example, FERRET can differentiate two texts about space probe launches if either the craft, the launch site, the destination, or the agency differ. But the JPL library of texts on the Voyager I mission, for example, might all be assigned the same abstract (the equivalent of "JPL sends Voyager I to Jupiter and Saturn"). Such domains will certainly require extensions to the basic knowledge representation scheme for such fine distinctions to be made. FERRET is an advance over keyword systems because it is able to make finer distinctions that simple word counting, but the granularity problem has not been solved; merely pushed back one level of detail.

Finally, Recall that the MCFRUMP parser is simpler than than the original FRUMP parser. In particular it has a far less powerful inference component than did FRUMP, and uses less detailed sketchy scripts in its knowledge representation. If the inference capability of the original FRUMP was restored and a more detailed database of sketchy scripts were added to MCFRUMP, that could improve FERRET's coverage and retrieval performance even more.

7.3.5. Storage Requirements

The newest medium for publishing texts is the CD ROM. A single laser disk can hold 500 megabytes of information (this book, including text and graphics, takes slightly over one megabyte of disk space). But often about half of that space is used for an inverted file so that the end user can access the text quickly using keywords (the inverted file is about the same size as the text).

---

*Personal communication.

In the same manner, the abstract database from FERRET could be stored along with the inverted word list, so that the CD ROM could be used by standard keyword retrieval systems, a FERRET style conceptual retrieval system, or a hybrid of the two. Table 7-4 shows the compressed and uncompressed sizes of the STARDATE text database, along with the inverted word list and the abstract database.

Sizes of Text and Index for STARDATE			
	Raw	Comp.	Percent of Original
StarDate texts:	1988k	728k	36.6%
Abstract, basic:	1172k	273k	23.3%
Abstract, learned:	2472k	583k	23.6%
Inverted file:	3152k	1307k	41.5%
Reduced Inverted file	1464k	631k	43.1%

Figure 7-4: Sizes of text and indices for STARDATE texts

Where sizes for compressed data are given, the Lempel-Ziv tokenizing compression algorithm is used [Welch 84]. Recent research into data compression has shown that some structures (such as word lists) can be effectively compressed and still be used efficiently without decompression [Jacobson 89]. Assuming that the compressed word lists and abstract databases are still effective, 512 megabytes of raw English text could be stored on a 500 megabyte CD ROM with 37.5 percent of the space being compressed text, 30 percent the compressed FERRET abstracts, and 32.5 percent the compressed word lists for keyword indexing. That's enough for over 450 PhD theses.

7.3.6. Issues of Scale

As with any successful artificial intelligence project, it is important to ask whether the results can be "scaled up" to real-sized problems. There are three basic parts of FERRET that must be considered in scaling up:

   • Storage space requirements

- Computation time
- Linguistic and knowledge resources

In considering the computational resources, we first note that the data storage required for parsed abstracts is less than storage space for the texts themselves, so storing the abstracts is not in itself a problem. However, to provide fast retrieval, the suggested algorithm shown in Section 7.3.2 does require $O(N \log N)$ space to store the extended inverted file (which could mean that as much as 10 megabytes might be necessary to store the index for 1 megabyte of text). Future research in indexed data structures might result in an algorithm that does not require this factor of 10 expansion in storage, but in any case with increasing disk drive densities and capacities, storage is not a crippling problem.

Considering computation time, the current parser is very slow. But we believe it could be sped up quite a bit (our estimate is a factor between 10 and 100 based on previous experience with Lisp-based prototype systems). We also note that all of the algorithms used to parse the texts require CPU time in linear proportion to the amount of input text, so handling twice as much text means only waiting twice as long (or buying twice as many computers to do parsing in the same amount of time). This is in distinction to the Latent Semantic Indexing approach, for example, which requires $O(N^3)$ time (see Section 2.1.5). The parsing process can also proceed totally in parallel, allowing large multi-processors to achieve the elusive linear speed-up. So there is no effective limit on the amount of text that can be handled by a FERRET style retrieval system.

The toughest barrier to building a practical knowledge-based retrieval system is building the lexical and domain knowledge base. Although the FERRET system has demonstrated an ability to extend its knowledge base using on-line dictionaries and feedback from users, building and maintaining the knowledge base is still a formidable task. For the near future, only systems which process text within a limited domain will be practical. Within a domain, the effort to build a knowledge base is within the bounds of practicality, although there is also a need to maintain such a knowledge base by adding new terms and concepts to the system over time. FERRET assists in its own adaptation, but it cannot modify itself to read Biology texts starting with an Astronomy knowledge base, for example. The knowledge problem is shared by all knowledge-based systems: given the limitations of knowledge-free approaches to text, this is the price we will have to pay to build systems that use an understanding of text to provide more effective information retrieval.

7.4. Conclusion

The original goal of this work as given in Section 1.6 has almost been met. Only the maintenance requirement has not been demonstrated. The machine learning component described in Chapter 5 is powerful enough to improve the system's performance, but does not offer a fully automated knowledge base acquisition system. However, it does show that FERRET's learning method is capable of augmenting the hand-built knowledge needed for parsing, resulting in improved recall performance.

As shown in Chapter 6, the conceptual approach to information retrieval provides both increases in recall and precision, and that the computer is thus better able to retrieve texts that the user is seeking.

The sea of text being stored in computers must be made accessible. For computers to make that access possible, they will have to take over the burden of searching, and that will require them to understand the texts in some fundamental way. The case frame approach exemplified by this project is only one of many methods for implementing computer understanding, but the results of this study show that computers can achieve the necessary understanding and outperform simple key word retrieval systems. This is a fruitful path for future research.

Appendix A
SAMPLE DATA STRUCTURES

This appendix contains samples of the major data structures used in the FERRET system.

A.1. Sample Texts

The domain of this study was the USENET NETNEWS system. A brief overview of NETNEWS is [Smith, B. 89]. Figure A-1 shows the geographical extent of the USENET network, and Figure A-2 shows how rapidly the network is growing.

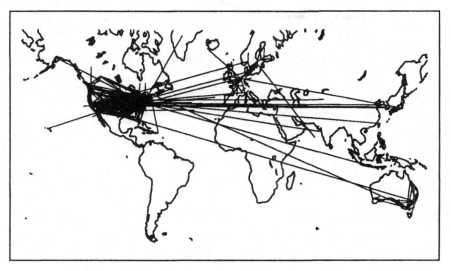

Figure A-1: UseNet as of April 15, 1989

Figures A-3 through A-5 show three sample articles from the SCI.ASTRO newsgroup. Figures A-6 through A-8 show these sample articles after processing by the text scanner.

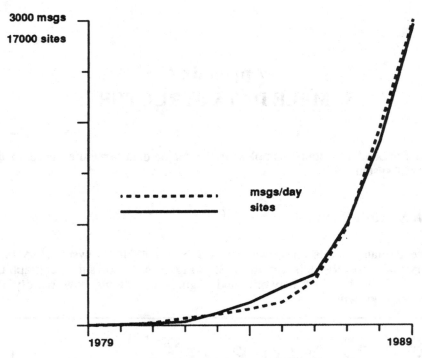

Figure A-2: USENET Growth, 1979-89

```
Article 1307 of 1351, Mar  3 02:00.
Subject: StarDate: March 3 Pioneer 10
From: dipper@utastro
Organization: U. Texas, Astronomy, Austin, TX
Newsgroups: net.astro
Date: Mon, 3-Mar-86 02:00:18 EST

Pioneer 10 was the first spacecraft to venture into the outer
solar system.  More -- coming up.

March 3  Pioneer 10

On today's date in the year 1972, NASA's Pioneer 10
spacecraft was launched toward the outer solar system.  It
was to become the first craft to travel beyond the asteroid
belt -- and the first to encounter mighty Jupiter.

Pioneer 10 is now on its way out of the solar system.  It is
now farther from the sun than any of the known planets --
still sampling the environment through which it moves -- and
still transmitting data back to Earth.

The spacecraft was originally designed for a mission lasting
21 months.  Its primary mission was to encounter Jupiter.

But the spacecraft has done much more.  Scientists used
Pioneer 10 data to go beyond the previous picture of the
solar system -- that of a central sun surrounded by a flat
disk of planets.  Thanks to Pioneer 10, we can now envision a
huge magnetic bubble containing the planets and sun -- a
bubble that may be streamlined into a teardrop as the sun at
its heart moves through the galaxy.  Some scientists also
think this bubble "breathes" -- expands and contracts -- with
each 11-year cycle of activity on the sun.

The outer boundary of the bubble is known as the heliopause,
the end of the sun's influence.  Outside the heliopause lies
the unsampled gas and dust of interstellar space.  Although
no one knows exactly when it will happen, Pioneer 10 will be
the first craft from Earth to cross the heliopause -- and
venture into the galaxy at large.

Script by Deborah Byrd.
(c) Copyright 1985, 1986 McDonald Observatory,
University of Texas at Austin
```

Figure A-3: Sample Text from SCI.ASTRO - 1

```
Article 29 of 8 Mar 86.
Subject: StarDate: March 8 Volcanos on Io
From: dipper@utastro
Newsgroups: net.astro
Date: Sat, 8-Mar-86 02:00:29 EST

Jupiter's moon Io has active volcanos.  More on how they were
discovered -- after this.

March 8  Volcanos on Io

Since the dawn of the space age, scientists hoped for the
discovery of a world besides Earth that would be geologically
active.  On this date in the year 1979, they found one.  It
was the satellite of Jupiter known as Io.

The Voyager spacecraft photographed Io, in its flight past
Jupiter seven years ago.  The discovery of volcanos on Io was
made by Linda Morabito, a member of the Voyager optical
navigation team.  In a routine check of some photographs,
Morabito noticed a mushroom-shaped feature extending above
Io's surface.  The feature turned out to be a plume of dust
and gas, expelled from an active volcano.

Even as Voyager sped past Io, that world's volcanos were in
the process of erupting.  The number and force of the
volcanos prompted Voyager scientists to point out that Io
isn't just an active world -- it's even more active than
Earth.  The volcanic ash spews up so powerfully that it's
comparable to bullets shot from high-powered rifles.

It would be interesting to land a spacecraft on Io.  But that
possibility may not be within the realm of present
technology.  Jupiter's magnetic field bathes Io in deadly
radiation.  We don't know for sure, but a landing craft may
have its electronic equipment deadened by this intense
bombardment.  Still, Io's volcanos might help us learn more
about the geologic history of the Earth.  It makes Io one of
the most fascinating worlds in the solar system -- even if it
is a world where humans or their spacecraft may never go.

Script by Deborah Byrd.
(c) Copyright 1985, 1986 McDonald Observatory,
University of Texas at Austin
```

Figure A-4: Sample Text from SCI.ASTRO - 2

Article 80 of 31 Mar 86.
Subject: StarDate: March 31 The Launch of Luna 10
From: dipper@utastro
Newsgroups: net.astro
Date: Mon, 31-Mar-86 02:00:16 EST

The moon is the Earth's natural satellite. More on the first
artificial satellite for the moon -- after this.

March 31   The Launch of Luna 10

A satellite is an object in space orbiting around something
else -- usually something larger. A satellite can be
natural, like Earth's moon -- or it can be artificial, like a
weather or communications satellite.

Well, today is the twentieth anniversary of the the first
artificial "moon" for the moon -- the first artificial
satellite to orbit a world besides Earth. On today's date
in the year 1966 the Soviet Union launched Luna 10 -- the
mothership for the first lunar satellite.

Luna 10 passed within 48 thousand miles of the moon. The
satellite -- about five feet long and two and a half feet in
diameter -- was ejected into an orbit around the moon.

The Luna 10 satellite circled the moon a total of 460 times.
It sent back data on lunar magnetism and gravity -- and on
mascons -- actual concentrations of mass located beneath the
moon's surface. Mascons affect the orbits of satellites
circling the moon.

After two months of orbiting the moon, the satellite's
batteries failed -- and communications were lost. But that
year, 1966, was especially fruitful for the Soviet's moon
missions. They had soft-landed a craft on the moon for the
first time in January. Later that year they got back the
first television images of the moon's surface -- possibly
scouting out landing places for a Soviet manned lunar mission
-- which by the way has yet to occur.

Still, in 1966, the mood was high. The Soviets celebrated
Luna 10 by having the satellite play the Soviet national
anthem -- the "Internationale" -- as it became the first
artificial "moon" for the moon.

Script by Diana Hadley and Deborah Byrd.
(c) Copyright 1985, 1986 McDonald Observatory,
University of Texas at Austin

Figure A-5: Sample Text from SCI.ASTRO - 3

A.2. Sample Texts after Scanning

Figures A-6 through A-8 show the sample texts after they have been processed by the text scanner. Details of the scanner are given in Appendix D.

```
(article
    (file (star.8603))
    (line (85))
    (byte (3691))
    (subject (%cpt stardate %colon %cpt march 3 %cpt
            pioneer 10))
    (from (dipper %at-sign utastro))
    (newsgroups (net %period astro))
    (date (%cpt mon %comma 3 %dash %cpt mar %dash 86 02
            %colon 00 %colon 18 %cpt est))
    (lisp-date (time 1986 3 3 2 0 18))
    (text ((p 3829) %cpt pioneer (number 10) was the first
            spacecraft to venture into the outer solar system
            %period (s 3906) %cpt more %dash %dash coming up
            %period (p 3926) (time 1986 3 3 -1 -1 -1) %cpt
            pioneer (number 10) (p 3947) %cpt on (time 1972 3
            3 -1 -1 -1) %cpt nasa %apostrophe s %cpt pioneer
            (number 10) spacecraft was launched toward the
            outer solar system %period (s 4055) %cpt it was to
            become the first craft to travel beyond the
            asteroid belt %dash %dash and the first to
            encounter mighty %cpt jupiter %period (p 4170)
            %cpt pioneer (number 10) is now on its way out of
            the solar system %period (s 4225) %cpt it is now
            farther from the sun than any of the known planets
            %dash %dash still sampling the environment through
            which it moves %dash %dash and still transmitting
            data back to %cpt earth %period (p 4390) %cpt the
            spacecraft was originally designed for a mission
            lasting (number 21) months %period (s 4463) %cpt
            its primary mission was to encounter %cpt jupiter
            %period (p 4510) %cpt but the spacecraft has done
            much more %period (s 4550) %cpt scientists used
            %cpt pioneer (number 10) data to go beyond the
                            . . .
            (p 5362) %cpt script by %cpt deborah %cpt byrd
            %period (s 5386) %open-paren c %close-paren %cpt
            copyright (number 1985) %comma (number 1986) %cpt
            mcdonald %cpt observatory %comma %cpt university
            of %cpt texas at %cpt austin (p 5465) (e 5465))))
```

Figure A-6: Sample Text After Scanning - 1

```
(article
    (file (star.8603))
    (line (295))
    (byte (12676))
    (subject (%cpt stardate %colon %cpt march 8 %cpt volcanos
              on %cpt io))
    (from (dipper %at-sign utastro))
    (newsgroups (net %period astro))
    (date (%cpt sat %comma 8 %dash %cpt mar %dash 86 02
           %colon 00 %colon 29 %cpt est))
    (lisp-date (time 1986 3 8 2 0 29))
    (text ((p 12819) %cpt jupiter %apostrophe s moon %cpt io
           has active volcanos %period (s 12859) %cpt more on
           how they were discovered %dash %dash after this
           %period (p 12908) (time 1986 3 8 -1 -1 -1) %cpt
           volcanos on %cpt io (p 12933) %cpt since the dawn
           of the space age %comma scientists hoped for the
           discovery of a world besides %cpt earth that would
           be geologically active %period (s 13062) %cpt on
           (time 1979 3 8 -1 -1 -1) they found one %period (s
           13110) %cpt it was the satellite of %cpt jupiter
           known as %cpt io %period (p 13156) %cpt the %cpt
           voyager spacecraft photographed %cpt io %comma in
           its flight past %cpt jupiter (number 7) years ago
           %period (s 13241) %cpt the discovery of volcanos
           on %cpt io was made by %cpt linda %cpt morabito
           %comma a member of the %cpt voyager optical
           navigation team %period (s 13351) %cpt in a
           routine check of some photographs %comma %cpt
           morabito noticed a mushroom %dash shaped feature
           extending above %cpt io %apostrophe s surface
           %period (s 13465) %cpt the feature turned out to
           be a plume of dust and gas %comma expelled from an
           active volcano %period (p 13553) %cpt even as %cpt
           voyager sped past %cpt io %comma that world
           %apostrophe s volcanos were in the process of
           erupting %period (s 13639) %cpt the number and
           force of the volcanos prompted %cpt voyager
           scientists to point out that %cpt io isn
           %apostrophe t just an active world %dash %dash it
           %apostrophe s even more active than %cpt earth
           %period (s 13790) %cpt the volcanic ash spews up
           so powerfully that it %apostrophe s comparable to
                        . . .
           script by %cpt deborah %cpt byrd %period (s 14445)
           %open-paren c %close-paren %cpt copyright (number
           1985) %comma (number 1986) %cpt mcdonald %cpt
           observatory %comma %cpt university of %cpt texas
           at %cpt austin (p 14524) (e 14524))))
```

Figure A-7: Sample Text After Scanning - 2

```
(article
    (file (star.8603))
    (line (853))
    (byte (36884))
    (subject (%cpt stardate %colon %cpt march 31 %cpt the
            %cpt launch of %cpt luna 10))
    (from (dipper %at-sign utastro))
    (newsgroups (net %period astro))
    (date (%cpt mon %comma 31 %dash %cpt mar %dash 86 02
            %colon 00 %colon 16 %cpt est))
    (lisp-date (time 1986 3 31 2 0 16))
    (text ((p 37037) %cpt the moon is the %cpt earth
            %apostrophe s natural satellite %period (s 37081)
            %cpt more on the first artificial satellite for
            the moon %dash %dash after this %period (p 37149)
            (time 1986 3 31 -1 -1 -1) %cpt the %cpt launch of
            %cpt luna 10 (p 37182) %cpt a satellite is an
            object in space orbiting around something else
            %dash %dash usually something larger %period (s
            37277) %cpt a satellite can be natural %comma like
            %cpt earth %apostrophe s moon %dash %dash or it
            can be artificial %comma like a weather or
            communications satellite %period (p 37396) %cpt
            well %comma (time 1986 3 31 -1 -1 -1) is the
            (ordinal 20) anniversary of the the first
            artificial %quote moon %quote for the moon %dash
            %dash the first artificial satellite to orbit a
            world besides %cpt earth %period (s 37552) %cpt on
            (time 1966 3 31 -1 -1 -1) the %cpt soviet %cpt
            union launched %cpt luna (number 10) %dash %dash
            the mothership for the first lunar satellite
            %period (p 37669) %cpt luna (number 10) passed
            within (ordinal 48) ousand miles of the moon
            %period (s 37723) %cpt the satellite %dash %dash
            about (number 5) feet long and (number 2) a half
            feet in diameter %dash %dash was ejected into an
            orbit around the moon %period (p 37844) %cpt the
            %cpt luna 10 satellite circled the moon a total of
            (number 460) times %period (s 37906) %cpt it sent
            back data on lunar magnetism and gravity %dash
            %dash and on mascons %dash %dash actual
            concentrations of mass located beneath the moon
                        ...
            %period (p 38759) %cpt script by %cpt diana %cpt
            hadley and %cpt deborah %cpt byrd %period (s
            38800) %open-paren c %close-paren %cpt copyright
            (number 1985) %comma (number 1986) %cpt mcdonald
            %cpt observatory %comma %cpt university of %cpt
            texas at %cpt austin (p 38877) (e 38878))))
```

Figure A-8: Sample Text After Scanning - 3

A.3. Sample Lexical Entries

The lexical knowledge is stored in FRAMEKIT frames, and there are, on average, three frames for a typical noun and two for a verb. The breakdown is as follows:

   12,281 total frames
    3,369 conceptual entries ("noun" in the type hierarchy)
    2,148 proper names
      376 basic verb entries (structure building words)

Figure A-9 shows some examples of lexical entries, including English tokens, phrases, word senses, conceptual entries, and structure building words. Figure A-10 shows a barely legible graph of the entire type hierarchy structure (except for the leaves). As is plainly visible, the hierarchy is quite bushy and the maximum depth is 10.

```
(pioneer
    (phrase
        (nil (*number* spacecraft) pioneer-spacecraft)
        (nil (spacecraft) pioneer-spacecraft)
        (nil (*number*) pioneer-spacecraft)))

(pioneer-spacecraft (senses pioneer-spacecraft1))

(pioneer-spacecraft1 (conent *pioneer-spacecraft*) (pos noun))

(*pioneer-spacecraft*
    (is-a *spacecraft*)
    (proper-name t)
    (elex (%cpt pioneer))
    (nationality *usa*)
    (affiliation *usa*))

(*spacecraft*
    (is-a *outer-space-location* *military-unit* *vehicle*)
    (elex (spacecraft))
    (inv+is-a *alouette1* *mir1* *salyut1* *veneral*
     *vega-probe1* *soyuz1* *shuttle1* *iras-satellite*
     *palaba-satellite* *westar-satellite*
     *telstar-satellite* *intelsat-satellite*
     *explorer-satellite* *voyager-probe*
     *surveyor-spacecraft* *pioneer-spacecraft*
     *discoverer-spacecraft* *luna-spacecraft*
     *viking-spacecraft* *mariner-spacecraft*))
```

Figure A-9: Sample Lexical Entries

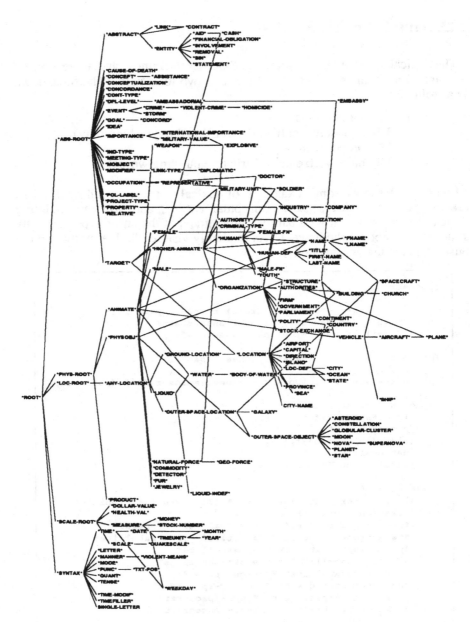

Figure A-10: The FERRET Type Hierarchy

A.4. Webster's Seventh Dictionary

The *Webster's Seventh Dictionary* was obtained from the G. & C. Merriam Company as a typesetting tape coded in EBCDIC, as described in [Peterson 82]. This dictionary contains the following numbers of items:

> 68,766 words
> 19,123 related words
> 6,740   variants
> 3,216   plurals
> 58,197 synonym entries
> 28,323 senses defined as synonyms

The original format was converted for use at Carnegie Mellon by the following steps:

- ASCII code was used instead of EBCDIC
- The continuation cards used in the original file were collapsed into single lines of varying length.
- The IBM typesetting codes were converted to a Scribe[*]-like notation, using "@i<*text*>" for italics, "@c" for small caps, and other Scribe macros for various diacritical marks.

Figure A-11 shows the definitions of "outer," "solar" and "venture" from *Webster's*. Figure A-12 shows the same definitions in the ASCII format, and Figure A-13 shows them after conversion to Lisp case frames by the DFMT program.

---

[*]Scribe[tm] is a trademark of Unilogic, Inc.

---

out·er (aut-*er*) aj. [ME, fr. ³*out* + *-er*, compar. suffix] 1. EXTERNAL, OBJECTIVE 2. a) situated farther out b) being away from a center.

so·lar ('sō-ler) aj. [ME, fr. L *solaris*, fr. *sol* sun; akin to OE & ON *sōl*

sun, Gk *hēlios*] 1. of, derived from, or relating to the sun esp. as affecting the earth 2. measured by the earth's course in relation to the sun <~ time ~ year>; *also* :: relating to or reckoned by solar time 3. produced or operated by the action of the sun's light or heat; *also* :: utilizing the sun's rays.

ven·ture¹ ('ven-cher) vb. **ven·tur·ing** ('vench-(e-)riŋ) [ME *venteren*, by shortening & alter. fr. *aventuren*, fr. *aventure* adventure] —vt. 1. to expose to hazard :: RISK 2. to undertake the risks and dangers of :: BRAVE 3. to offer at the risk of rebuff, rejection, or censure —vi. 1. to proceed despite danger :: DARE.

venture² n. 1. *obs* FORTUNE, CHANCE 2. a) an undertaking involving chance, risk, or danger; *esp* :: a speculative business enterprise b) a venturesome act 3. something at hazard in a speculative venture (as a trading ship or its cargo) **at a venture** 1. at hazard or random

---

Figure A-11: Sample Definition as typeset

```
F:outer;;;3;;aj;;
P:a{u.}t-*r
E:ME, fr. @+<3>@i<out> + @i<-er>, compar. suffix
D:1;;;aj;@c<EXTERNAL>, @c<OBJECTIVE>
D:2;a;;aj;situated farther out
D:2;b;;aj;being away from a center
F:solar;;;2;;aj;;
P:'s{o-}-l*r
E:ME, fr. L @i<solaris>, fr. @i<sol> sun; akin to
  OE & ON @i<s{o-}l> sun, Gk @i<h{e-}lios>
D:1;;;aj;of, derived from, or relating to the sun
  esp. as affecting the earth
D:2;;;aj;measured by the earth's course in relation
  to the sun <_ time _ year>; @i<also> :: relating
  to or reckoned by solar time
D:3;;;aj;produced or operated by the action of the
  sun's light or heat; @i<also> :: utilizing the
  sun's rays
F:venture;1;;3;;vb;;
P:'ven-ch*r
V:venturing;33;;11
P:'vench-(*-)ri{n_}
E:ME @i<venteren>, by shortening & alter. fr.
  @i<aventuren>, fr. @i<aventure> adventure
D:1;;;vt;to expose to hazard :: @c<RISK>
D:2;;;vt;to undertake the risks and dangers of ::
  @c<BRAVE>
D:3;;;vt;to offer at the risk of rebuff, rejection,
  or censure
D:0;;;vi;to proceed despite danger :: @c<DARE>
F:venture;2;;;;n;;
L:1;;;@i<obs>
D:1;;;n;@c<FORTUNE>, @c<CHANCE>
D:2;a;;n;an undertaking involving chance, risk, or
  danger; @i<esp> :: a speculative business
  enterprise
D:2;b;;n;a venturesome act
D:3;;;n;something at hazard in a speculative
  venture (as a trading ship or its cargo)
R:at a venture;;;;;
D:0;;;n;at hazard or random
```

Figure A-12: Sample Definition from Webster's File

```
(outer (senses w7-outer))
(w7-outer
    (pos adjective)
    (synonym (external objective))
    (definition (situated farther out)
                (being away from a center)))

(solar (senses w7-solar))
(w7-solar
    (pos adjective)
    (definition
        (of %comma derived from %comma or relating to the sun
         esp %period as affecting the earth)
        (measured by the earth %apostrophe s course in relation
         to the sun %open-angle %underscore time %underscore
         year %close-angle %semi-colon also %colon %colon
         relating to or reckoned by solar time)
        (produced or operated by the action of the sun
         %apostrophe s light or heat %semi-colon also %colon
         %colon utilizing the sun %apostrophe s rays)))

(venture (senses w7-venture-1))
(venturing (senses (w7-venture-1 ger)))
(w7-venture-1
    (pos verb)
    (variant (venturing ger))
    (synonym (risk) (brave) (dare))
    (definition
        (to expose to hazard %colon %colon risk)
        (to undertake the risks and dangers of %colon %colon
         brave)
        (to offer at the risk of rebuff %comma rejection %comma
         or censure)
        (to proceed despite danger %colon %colon dare)))
(venture (senses w7-venture-2))
(at-a-venture (related w7-venture-2))
(at (phrase (nil (a venture) at-a-venture)))
(w7-venture-2
    (pos noun)
    (synonym (fortune chance))
    (definition
        (an undertaking involving chance %comma risk %comma or
         danger %semi-colon esp %colon %colon a speculative
         business enterprise)
        (a venturesome act)
        (something at hazard in a speculative venture
         %open-paren as a trading ship or its cargo %close-paren)
        (at hazard or random))
    (related (at-a-venture))))
```

Figure A-13: Sample Definitions Converted to Lisp Format

A.5. Sample Sketchy Scripts

```
(script
    (bnego-r1
        (graph
            (cd (actor (:req &side1 *organization*))
                (is (*link* (type (*negotiation*))))
                (with (:req &side2 *organization*))
                (time (*tf*))))
        (init (t))
        (causals ((leadto bnego-r2)))
        (constraints ((different (actor) (with))))))
(script
    (vehac-r1
        (graph
            (cd (actor (:req &obj1 *vehicle*))
                (<=> (*propel*))
                (object (:req &obj2 *physobj*))
                (loc (:opt &loc *loc-def*))))
        (init (t))))
(script
    (outer-space-motion-r1
        (graph
            (cd (actor    (:req &move-object
                               *outer-space-object*))
                (<=>      (*ptrans*))
                (object   (:req &move-object
                               *outer-space-object*))
                (from     (:req &move-source
                               *outer-space-location*))
                (to       (:opt &move-dest
                               *outer-space-location*))
                (time     (:opt &move-date *time*))
                (mode     (:opt &move-mode *mode*))))
        (init (t))
        (constraints (  (different (from) (to))
                        (different (actor) (from))
                        (different (actor (to)))))))
(script
    (astro-view-r1
        (graph
            (cd (actor    (:req &viewer *higher-animate*))
                (<=>      (*perceive*))
                (object   (:req &view-object
                               *outer-space-object*))
                (inst     (:opt &view-inst *detector*))
                (loc      (:opt &view-loc *any-location*))
                (time     (:opt &view-date *time*))
                (mode     (:opt &view-mode nil))))
        (init (t))))
```

Figure A-14: Sample Sketchy Scripts

A.6. Sample Texts after Parsing

```
((reference (file f500/star.8603) (line 39) (byte 1739))
 (launch-r2
     (&spacecraft (*pioneer-spacecraft*))
     (&launch-dest
         (*solar-system* (type (w7-outer))
                         (ref (def)))))
 (cd
     (<=> (*ptrans*))
     (actor (*pioneer-spacecraft*))
     (object (*pioneer-spacecraft*))
     (to (*solar-system* (type (w7-outer))
                         (ref (def)))))
 (p-1875 pioneer-spacecraft was the first spacecraft to
  venture into the outer solar-system %period))
```

Figure A-15: Abstract from Sample Text

A.7. Sample Retrieval

```
Ferret,  1-Apr-89, from Franz Lisp, Opus 38

1.ferret
                  Top level interface to Ferret

Show sentences too [y/n]: y

Enter CD pattern: (cd (actor (*spacecraft*))
                      (to (*solar-system*)))
[ Found 2 articles ]

Articles matching
(cd (actor (*spacecraft*)) (to (*solar-system*)))

  1] StarDate: January 5  On the Way to the Heliopause
     ((Only 4 spacecraft from Earth have ever gone toward
        the outer solar-system -- toward the giant planets
        Jupiter %c Saturn %c Uranus and Neptune))
  2] StarDate: March 3  Pioneer 10
     ((pioneer-spacecraft was the first spacecraft to
        venture into the outer solar-system))

Choice (or 'q' to quit): 2
[ Use the editor to see f500/star.8603, line 39.
  Type ^C to return ]
```

window with original text pops up on Screen

Figure A-16: Sample Retrieval

```
Choice (or 'q' to quit): a 2
Abstract: ((reference (file f500/star.8603)
                      (line 39) (byte 1739))
          (launch-r2
             (&spacecraft (*pioneer-spacecraft*))
             (&launch-dest
                (*solar-system* (type (w7-outer))
                                (ref (def)))))
          (cd
             (<=> (*ptrans*))
             (actor (*pioneer-spacecraft*))
             (object (*pioneer-spacecraft*))
             (to (*solar-system* (type (w7-outer))
                                 (ref (def)))))
          (p-1875 pioneer-spacecraft was the first
           spacecraft to venture into the outer
           solar-system %period))

Choice (or 'q' to quit): q

Enter CD pattern: q
goodbye
```

Figure A-16: Sample Retrieval

Appendix B
USER QUERIES USED IN THE STUDIES

B.1. Sample User Survey Form

```
FERRET User query survey form, #1397 Mon Mar 20 19:43:54 1989

            Please read these three paragraphs.

Paragraph 1      _X__            File ID s500/star.8710, 17814
If you could see a map of the solar system this month -- one
that showed the planets in their orbits -- you'd see that
Mars is now far ahead of Earth in its orbit -- nearly on the
other side of the sun.  Mars moves more slowly than we do.
So our motion, not the motion of Mars, will bring the planet
nearer -- and cause it to be in our sky for a longer and
longer time each night.  We'll catch up to Mars -- and pass
between it and the sun -- next September.

Paragraph 2      _X__            File ID f500/star.8604, 13238
But there's one star that never moves -- at least it doesn't
move very much -- because it's located almost exactly at the
northernmost point around which the ball turns.  If Earth's
axis really were a long stick that could be extended
indefinitely, it would almost touch this north star.

Paragraph 3      ____            File ID f500/star.8501, 5409
A star in the winter sky is one of the largest stars known.
More on Betelgeuse -- after this.
```

Think of a question about astronomy to which one or more of
these paragraphs is relevant. Imagine that you must give
your question to a librarian who searches through the
astronomy database and finds these paragraphs (and possibly
many more) that are relevant to your question. Write your
query in normal conversational English on the line below.

Your query: *When and where in the sky is Mars visible?*

Now think of how you would formulate your query for a library
card catalog system. Use the form of the system that you are
most familiar with, or simply chose keywords that you think
should work. Write this version of your query on the line
below.

Keyword version of your query:
Mars, position, visibility

Finally, go back and put a check mark on the line above each
of the paragraphs that you consider relevant to your query.

B.2. User Queries Used in the Study

This is a complete list of all user queries obtained using the survey forms. Below each sentence, in all caps, is the paraphrase (if any) given to the MCFRUMP query parser. In some cases, the sentences were not paraphrased, in many the sentences were not understood at all. Where pronouns occur in the query, they refer to the previous query.

1. I want to find out about stars that vary in brightness over time.
   PARSED AS IS

2. Find examples of planets that radiate energy.
   PLANETS SHINE

3. What are the types of phases of the moon?
   MOON CHANGING PHASES, *parse horribly misunderstood*

4. Info about the way the night sky looks at different times of the year, or from different locations.
   NOT PARSED

5. Info about the solar system, the planets, and explorations of it.
   PROBES VISIT PLANETS

6. What is Newton's law of Universiality?
   NOT PARSED

7. Where is the Orion Nebula?
   YOU CAN SEE THE ORION NEBULA

8. When has Halley's Comet appeared?
   PARSED AS IS

9. How long does it [take] Earth to travel the distance between the Earth and the moon?
   PARSED AS IS, *parse horribly misunderstood*

10. What elements make up the atmosphere of Mercury?
    ANYTHING ABOUT MERCURY, *Ferret can't represent atmosphere*

11. Would Voyager 2 answer the question of whether or not Neptune has rings?
    VOYAGER 2 VISITS NEPTUNE

12. What is the magnitude of Sirius in Canis Major?
    YOU CAN SEE SIRIUS

13. What is its maximum declination and when does it occur?
    WHEN CAN YOU CAN SEE SIRIUS AT MAXIMUM DECLINATION?

14. How can you tell the age of a star, in gross terms (i.e. very old or not so old)?
    NOT PARSED

15. What are some interesting astronomical observations which have been carried out by non-professional astronomers in the past 50 years?
    NOT PARSED

16. Other than the sun and moon, what astronomical objects have the greatest apparent brightness?
    NOT PARSED

17. How can we gain information about the chemical composition of cosmological objects which may not be directly observable?
    NOT PARSED

18. In what manner have new planets been discovered?
    HOW DO PEOPLE DISCOVER PLANETS?

19. Why do stars twinkle but planets don't?
    PARSED AS IS

20. What are the fuzzy patches of brightness in the night sky?
    NOT PARSED

21. What was the outermost planet in 1972, Pluto or Neptune?
    NOT PARSED

22. I'm going camping on the 21st. Are there any meteor showers expected around then, or other interesting things to look for? What's the best time of day and direction to look for meteors?
    NOT PARSED

23. What is known about the physical characteristics of the Gas giants and their moons?
    NOT PARSED

24. Produce material relevant to observing new astronomical phenomena.
    NOT PARSED

25. What were some of the events causing changes in the way astronomers thought about the solar system?
    NOT PARSED

26. Is the shape of a planet's orbit important?
    PLANETS ORBIT THE SUN

27. How do I find the constellation Gemini?
    PARSED AS IS

28. What are the remaining planetary encounters for the Voyager spacecraft, and when do they occur.
    VOYAGER VISITS THE PLANETS

29. What was the last planet or planetary satellite discovered in the eighteenth century, and who discovered it?
    PERSON DISCOVERED PLANET

30. When the space shuttle orbits the earth, how long does it take to go around once?
    HOW DOES THE SPACE SHUTTLE ORBIT THE EARTH?

31. What are some astrological phenomenon that are visible in the night sky?
    NOT PARSED, *lots of paraphrases would work, but would retrieve the whole database*

32. What are some theories about comets, origins of meteorites, and the amount of matter in the universe
    WHERE CAN I SEE COMETS?

33. What other uses of absorption spectra are there in astronomy?
    NOT PARSED

34. What accounts for the luminance of asteroids, comets, and meteors?
    NOT PARSED

35. What is the origin of the signs of the zodiac?
    NOT PARSED

36. What kinds of radiation may be associated with black holes?
    NOT PARSED

37. I need to find a reference on planetary nebula formation
    NOT PARSED

38. I'd like references on how ancient peoples (before, say 1200 AD) constructed calendars (e.g. using the summer solstice, or vernal equinox)
    NOT PARSED

39. When and where in the sky is Mars visible?
    WHEN CAN I SEE MARS?

40. What evidence has convinced scientists that black holes do indeed exist?
    NOT PARSED

41. Please give me information on early landings on nearby planets.

PROBES VISIT NEARBY PLANETS, *nearby was mapped to Mercury,
Venus and Mars*

42. Find an explanation of why our sky is blue.
    NOT PARSED

43. At what time should I look for Saturn next week?
    PARSED AS IS

44. In what direction is the center of the galaxy?
    NOT PARSED

Appendix C
RAW DATA FOR EMPIRICAL STUDIES

This section gives the retrieval results for each query parsed. There are 5 columns of numbers, the first is the total number of texts retrieved from the training database in response to the query. The second column is the number of retrieved texts from the training database that were in fact considered relevant to the query. The third and fourth columns are the retrieved and relevant texts from the evaluation database. Five of the queries have a fifth column: these were part of the sample for the study of absolute recall described in Section 6.4.7. The fifth column shows the total number of relevant texts retrieved by exhaustive manual search of the evaluation database.

```
(p-120 %cpt i want to find out about stars that vary in
 brightness over time %period)
```

CD query:	59	1	69	1	
Keyword:	1	0	0	0	
Learn:	122	1	168	3	

```
(p-341 %cpt find examples of planets that radiate energy
 %period)
```

CD query:	4	2	5	1	
Keyword:	0	0	0	0	
Learn:	5	2	10	5	7

```
(p-566 %cpt moon changing phases %period)
```

CD query:	0	0	0	0
Keyword:	6	6	6	4
Eval:	0	0	0	0

```
(p-1194 %cpt probes visit planets %period)
```

CD query:	17	17	7	7
Keyword:	7	6	1	1
Learn:	19	19	7	7

```
(p-1561 %cpt you can see the %cpt orion %cpt nebula %period)
```

CD query:	2	2	1	1
Keyword:	3	3	3	3
Learn:	3	2	2	1

```
(p-1715 %cpt when has comet-halley appeared %question)
```

CD query:	7	7	3	3	
Keyword:	3	3	2	2	
Learn:	13	11	8	7	16

```
(p-1910 %cpt how long does it take %cpt earth to travel the
 distance between the %cpt earth and the-moon %question)
```

CD query:	0	0	0	0
Keyword:	13	0	20	0
Learn:	0	0	0	0

```
(p-2199 %cpt probe visit mercury %period (really about atmosphere))
```

CD query:	18	1	11	1
Keyword:	7	3	2	1
Learn:	20	1	17	2

```
(p-2445 voyager-probe visits %cpt neptune %period)
```

CD query:	2	2	3	1
Keyword:	6	5	2	1
Learn:	2	2	3	1

```
(p-2638 %cpt you can see %cpt sirius %period)
```

CD query:	1	1	2	2
Keyword:	1	1	0	0
Learn:	3	3	3	3

```
(p-2840 %cpt when can you can see %cpt sirius at maximum declination
%question)
```

CD query:	1	1	2	2
Keyword:	0	0	0	0
Learn:	3	1	3	3

```
(p-4188 %cpt how do people discover planets %question)
```

CD query:	8	2	10	4	
Keyword:	19	5	19	11	
Learn:	13	5	20	11	13

(p-4343 %cpt why do stars twinkle but planets do not %question)

CD query:	4	2	4	0
Keyword:	2	1	2	1
Learn:	9	3	9	1

(p-6077 %cpt planets orbit sol)

CD query:	15	10	19	16
Keyword:	0	0	1	1
Learn:	28	15	41	36

(p-6230 %cpt how do %cpt i find the const-gemini %question)

CD query:	0	0	0	0	
Keyword:	0	0	0	0	
Learn:	0	0	2	1	6

(p-6540 %cpt voyager visits the planets %period)

CD query:	8	8	2	2
Keyword:	0	0	0	0
Learn:	9	9	4	4

(p-6805 %cpt person discovered planet %period)

CD query:	8	0	10	1
Keyword:	0	0	0	0
Learn:	13	0	15	1

(p-7044 %cpt how does space-shuttle orbit the earth %question)

CD query:	0	0	0	0
Keyword:	0	0	0	0
Learn:	0	0	0	0

(p-7668 %cpt where can %cpt i see comets %question)

CD query:	14	1	15	12
Keyword:	0	0	0	0
Learn:	20	2	19	14

(p-9066 %cpt when can %cpt i see %cpt mars %question)

CD query:	14	11	16	12	
Keyword:	0	0	0	0	
Learn:	26	22	18	15	33

(p-9485 %cpt probes visit nearby planets %period)

CD query:	3	0	1	1
Keyword:	5	4	4	4
Learn:	4	0	3	1

(p-9825 %cpt at what time should %cpt i look for %cpt saturn
 next week %question)

```
CD query:      8       8            9       9
Keyword:       4       0            1       0
Learn:        15      12           13      11
```

Appendix D
THE NUMBER AND DATE GRAMMARS

This appendix gives parts of the LEX [Bell Labs 79] programs for SPECIAL and SCAN, the routines that do the lexical processing for FERRET. They identify numbers, dates, times, special lexical items, and punctuation. The output is a list of Lisp frames, one per input article, that can be more easily processed by the Lisp code for the MCFRUMP parser. Here is a brief list of the types of tokens in the output:

(special *type value*) A special token such as a phone-number or lat/lon pair.

(time *year month day hour minute second*)

A time and date specification. Omitted entries are represented by **-1**.

(number *value*)   a cardinal value (eg. "fifty three" becomes (**number 53**)).

(ordinal *value*)   an ordinal value (eg. "fifty third" becomes (**ordinal 53**)).

(fraction *num den*) a fractional value (eg. "fifty thirds" becomes (**fraction 50 3**)).

(p *byte*)   Start of paragraph, the value is the byte offset from the start of the file.

(s *byte*)   Start of sentence, the value is the byte offset from the start of the file.

(e *byte*)   End of file, the value is the byte offset from the start of the file.

%cpt   The next word was capitalized in the input.

%punc   Punctuation marks are mapped into tokens, such as **%period**, **%comma**, and **%dash**.

The number grammar has many rules, each of which calls one or more small C routines. The number is built up one piece at a time, and several variables hold various parts of the number:

r_1	Keeps current "hundreds" number. For example, in "two hundred twenty three thousand one hundred and thirty," the r_1 variable collects the "223" that modifies "thousand."
h_1	Is a boolean that tracks whether r_1 contains a number.
r_2	Is kept as a running total of the whole number. In the previous example, the value 223,000 is stored in r_2 while the parser reads the second half of the number.
h_2	Is a boolean that tracks whether r_1 contains a number.
scale	current scale, "hundreds," "thousands," "millions," etc.
lastmult	previous scale. When the new scale is is smaller, the result is additive (one thousand one hundred), when the new scale is larger, the result is multiplicative (one hundred thousand).

The grammar also extracts dates and times, and the text is collected into a string variable *datestr*. When the whole text of the data/time is collected, it is evaluated by the PARSEDATE library routine.[*]

The SPECIAL grammar extracts unusual tokens like stellar positions, lat/lon pairs, Email addresses or phone numbers. These have been specially marked and are passed through to the output stream.

Also, paragraph boundaries, sentence boundaries and end of file are marked with special tokens; each is Lisp pair containing a letter indicating the type of mark and a number which is the byte offset of the paragraph or sentence from the beginning of the file: (**p** *num*), (**s** *num*), and (**e** *num*).

There is currently a bug in the C routines, so that a number like "503 million" is parsed incorrectly. Using the phrase "Five hundred and three million" works properly.

---

[*]PARSEDATE is a Yacc program written at Carnegie Mellon University by Leonard Hamey that understands a variety of date forms such as "Next Wednesday," "3/23/59," or "Every Christmas."

The SPECIAL LEX Grammar

```
E           /[^a-zA-Z0-9\-]
INT         [0-9]+
INT3        [0-9][0-9][0-9]
INT4        [0-9][0-9][0-9][0-9]
YEAR        (the{W}year{W})?[112]{INT3}
ID          ([a-zA-Z][a-zA-Z0-9\-]*)
W           [ \t\n]+
O           [ \t\n]*
MONABR      (jan|feb|mar|apr|may|jun|jul|aug|sep|sept|oct|nov|dec|dec)
MONFUL      (january|february|march|april|may|june|july|august|september|\
              october|nov|november|december)
MON         ({MONABR}"."?|{MONFUL})
DH          (({INT})({O}(d|deg|degrees?|h|hours?))?)
DM          (({INT}{O}(m|min|minutes?|"'"))
DS          ((({INT}{O}(s|sec|seconds?|"\""))(".".{INT})?)
DG          [+-]?(({DH}({O}{DM}({O}{DS})?)?|({DM}({O}{DS})?)|{DS}|\
              (({INT}{O})*{INT}(".".{INT})?))
DEG         {DG}(({O}"+/-"{DG})?
OFFSET      {DG}{O}(n|e|w|s|north|south|east|west)(({O}"+/-"{DG})?

^"article "{INT}" of ".*$          { printf ("\s%s\", byte %d, line %d.",
                                             "\nArticle from \"",
                                             inputfile,
                                             yyftell()-yyleng,
                                             yylineno);
                                     inarticle=1; }
^[a-z][a-z0-9_.\-]+:              { ECHO; }

({MON}{O})?{INT}"."{INT}{O}ut{E} { special ("utime", yytext); }
("("({INT3})")"{O})?(({INT3})"-"({INT4})({O}[x/]({INT4}))*           |
({INT3})"-"({INT3})"-"({INT4})({O}[x/]({INT4}))* {
                                   special ("phone", yytext); }
({INT3})"-"([0-9][0-9])"-"({INT4}) { special ("soc", yytext); }
("{"{ID}([,|]{O}{ID})*"}")|({ID}("."{ID})*)([%]{ID}("."{ID})*)+ {
                                   special ("email", yytext); }
"<"{INT}([%]{ID}("."{ID})*)+">" { special ("artid", yytext); }
{INT}("."{INT})?(e[+-]?{INT})?   { ECHO; }
{OFFSET}[ ,/]+{OFFSET}{E}        { special ("latlon", yytext); }
r[.]?a[.]?{O}(={O})?{DEG}[, \t\n]*decl?[.]?{O}\
   (={O})?{DEG}({O}"("equ[^)]*")")?{E}  {
                                   special ("stpos", yytext); }

[a-z]+"-"\n" "*[a-z]+            { register char *s;
                                   for (s=yytext; *s; s++)
                                   { if (*s != '-' &&
                                         *s != '\n' &&
                                         *s != ' ')
                                     { putchar (*s); }
                                   }
```

```
                                        }

/* Mark sentence and paragraph boundaries */

[.!?]([ \t]*\n)([ \t]*\n)+        { printf ("%c", *yytext);
                                    if (inarticle)
                                    { printf (" (&p %d) ", yyftell()); }
                                    else
                                    { printf ("\n\n"); }
                                  }

[.!?](\n|" "|\t)[ \t]*            { printf ("%c", *yytext);
                                    if (inarticle)
                                    { printf (" (&p %d) ", yyftell()); }
                                  }

^([ \t]*\n)+                      { if (inarticle)
                                    { printf (" (&p %d) ", yyftell()); }
                                  }

{ID}                              |
\n                                |
.                                 { ECHO; }
```

The SCAN LEX Grammar

```
/* Lex macros */

BAR      [\-=~*#%+
EW       /[^a-zA-Z0-9\-]
INT      [0-9]+
INT2     ([0-9][0-9])
INT3     ([0-9][0-9][0-9])
INT4     ([0-9][0-9][0-9][0-9])
ID       ([a-zA-Z][a-zA-Z0-9\-]*)
YEAR     (the{W}year{W})?[112][0-91][0-91][0-91]
W        [ \t\n]+
OW       [ \t\n]*
MONABR   (jan|feb|mar|apr|may|jun|jul|aug|sep|sept|oct|nov|dec|dec)
MONFUL   (january|february|march|april|may|june|july|august|september|\
          october|nov|november|december)
MON      ({MONABR}"."?|{MONFUL})
DAYABR   (sun|mon|tue|wed|thu|fri|sat)
DAYFUL   (sunday|monday|tuesday|wednesday|thursday|friday|saturday)
CARD12   (one|two|three|four|five|six|seven|eight|nine|ten|eleven|\
          twelve)
CARD19   ({CARD12}|thirteen|fourteen|fifteen|sixteen|seventeen|\
          eighteen|nineteen)
ORD9     (first|second|third|fourth|fifth|sixth|seventh|eighth|ninth)
```

```
ORD19    ({ORD9}|{CARD19}th)
DATENUM  (({INT}(st|nd|rd|th)?)|{ORD19})
TIMEMOD  (am|pm|noon|midnight|(in{W}the{W})?(morning|evening|\
         afternoon)|o"'"?clock)
QSTR     ["]([^"]|"\\".)*["]

/* Lex rules - article location */

"("special{W}{ID}{W}{QSTR}")"    { FLUSH special (yytext); }
"(&"[a-z]" "{INT}")"{OW}         { FLUSH
                                   if (sscanf (yytext+4, "%d", &pos))
                                     marker (yytext[2], pos); }
^[-]+"\nnewsgroup "[a-z.]+\n[-]+\n { FLUSH
                                   if (!inspec)
                                     marker ('e', yyftell()-yyleng);
                                   newsgroup (yytext); }
^"article "{INT}" of ".*\n       { FLUSH
                                   inspec=0;
                                   marker ('e', yyftell()-yyleng);
                                   article (yytext,
                                            inputfile,
                                            yyftell()-yyleng,
                                            yylineno); }

^"article from "{QSTR}", byte "{INT}", line "{INT}"."\n {
                                   FLUSH
                                   inspec=1;
                                   specialarticle (yytext); }
^date:{W}.*\n                    { FLUSH
                                   now = atot (yytext+6);
                                   header (yytext);
                                 }
^[a-z][a-z0-9_.\-]+:" ".*\n      { FLUSH header (yytext); }
^[ \t]*{BAR}{BAR}{BAR}*[ \t]*\n  { FLUSH bartext (); }
^[*>\]][ *>\]]*.*\n              { FLUSH refer (yytext); }

/* The number grammar */

one{W}second{EW}                         { if (innumber ())
                                           { adddigit (1);
                                             FLUSH
                                             dotext ("second");
                                           }
                                           else
                                           { dotext (yytext); }
                                         }

ones?               { adddigit (1); }
twos?               { adddigit (2); }
threes?             { adddigit (3); }
fours?              { adddigit (4); }
fives?              { adddigit (5); }
sixs?               { adddigit (6); }
sevens?             { adddigit (7); }
```

```
eights?                    { adddigit (8); }
nines?                     { adddigit (9); }
zeros?                     { adddigit (0); }
tens?                      { addteen (10); }
elevens?                   { addteen (11); }
twelves?                   { addteen (12); }
thirteens?                 { addteen (13); }
fourteens?                 { addteen (14); }
fifteens?                  { addteen (15); }
sixteens?                  { addteen (16); }
seventeens?                { addteen (17); }
eighteens?                 { addteen (18); }
nineteens?                 { addteen (19); }
score                      { if (innumber ())
                               addmult (20.0);
                             else
                               dotext (yytext); }

hundreds?                  { addmult (100.0); }
thousands?                 { addmult (1000.0); }
millions?                  { addmult (1.0e6); }
billions?                  { addmult (1.0e9); }
trillions?                 { addmult (1.0e12); }
twent(y|ies)               { addenty (20); }
thirt(y|ies)               { addenty (30); }
fourt(y|ies)               { addenty (40); }
fift(y|ies)                { addenty (50); }
sixt(y|ies)                { addenty (60); }
sevent(y|ies)              { addenty (70); }
eight(y|ies)               { addenty (80); }
ninet(y|ies)               { addenty (90); }

firsts                     { FLUSH dotext (yytext); }
first                      { orddigit (1, 0); }
seconds                    { FLUSH dotext (yytext); }
second                     { orddigit (2, 0); }
halves                     { orddigit (2, 1); }
thirds?                    { orddigit (3, yytext[yyleng-1] == 's'); }
fourths?                   { orddigit (4, yytext[yyleng-1] == 's'); }
fifths?                    { orddigit (5, yytext[yyleng-1] == 's'); }
sixths?                    { orddigit (6, yytext[yyleng-1] == 's'); }
sevenths?                  { orddigit (7, yytext[yyleng-1] == 's'); }
eighths?                   { orddigit (8, yytext[yyleng-1] == 's'); }
ninths?                    { orddigit (9, yytext[yyleng-1] == 's'); }
zeroths?                   { orddigit (0, yytext[yyleng-1] == 's'); }
tenths?                    { ordteen (10, yytext[yyleng-1] == 's'); }
elevenths?                 { ordteen (11, yytext[yyleng-1] == 's'); }
twelfths?                  { ordteen (12, yytext[yyleng-1] == 's'); }
thirteenths?               { ordteen (13, yytext[yyleng-1] == 's'); }
fourteenths?               { ordteen (14, yytext[yyleng-1] == 's'); }
fifteenths?                { ordteen (15, yytext[yyleng-1] == 's'); }
sixteenths?                { ordteen (16, yytext[yyleng-1] == 's'); }
seventeenths?              { ordteen (17, yytext[yyleng-1] == 's'); }
eighteenths?               { ordteen (18, yytext[yyleng-1] == 's'); }
```

```
nineteenths?              { ordteen (19, yytext[yyleng-1] == 's'); }
hundredths?               { ordmult (100.0,  yytext[yyleng-1] == 's'); }
thousandths?              { ordmult (1000.0, yytext[yyleng-1] == 's'); }
millionths?               { ordmult (1.0e6,  yytext[yyleng-1] == 's'); }
billionths?               { ordmult (1.0e9,  yytext[yyleng-1] == 's'); }
trillionths?              { ordmult (1.0e12, yytext[yyleng-1] == 's'); }
twentieths?               { ordenty (20, yytext[yyleng-1] == 's'); }
thirtieths?               { ordenty (30, yytext[yyleng-1] == 's'); }
fourtieths?               { ordenty (40, yytext[yyleng-1] == 's'); }
fiftieths?                { ordenty (50, yytext[yyleng-1] == 's'); }
sixtieths?                { ordenty (60, yytext[yyleng-1] == 's'); }
seventieths?              { ordenty (70, yytext[yyleng-1] == 's'); }
eightieths?               { ordenty (80, yytext[yyleng-1] == 's'); }
ninetieths?               { ordenty (90, yytext[yyleng-1] == 's'); }

"--"                      { FLUSH dotext (yytext); }
[ ,\-\t]+                 { if (havedate)              ADDDATE;
                            else if (!innumber ()) dotext (yytext); }
and{EW}                   { if (! innumber ())
                            { FLUSH dotext (yytext); }}
[+-]?{INT}("."{INT})?(e[+-]?{INT})? {
                            FLUSH setnum (atof (yytext)); FLUSH }
{INT}                     { setnum (atof (yytext)); }
","{INT3}/[^0-9]          { addtrip (atoi (yytext+1)); }
[0-9]*1[ ]*sts?           |
[0-9]*2[ ]*nds?           |
[0-9]*3[ ]*rds?           |
[0-9]*[4-90][ ]*ths?      { if (innumber ())
                            { dofraction (getnum (), atof (yytext)); }
                            else
                            { setnum (atof (yytext)); ordinal (); }
                          }
{INT}-{INT}               { int num, den;
                            if (sscanf (yytext, "%d-%d", &num, &den))
                            { dofraction ((double) num, (double) den); }
                            else
                            { dotext (yytext); }
                          }

/* Date and time grammar */

the{W}{ORD19}({W}day)?{W}of{W}{MON}{EW} |
{MON}{W}{DATENUM}                       { ADDDATE; havedate++; noyear++; }
{INT}(:{INT})+({OW}{TIMEMOD})?{EW}      |
{DAYFUL}({OW}{TIMEMOD})?{EW}            |
({INT}|{CARD12}){OW}{TIMEMOD}{EW}       |
(this|next|last){W}((({DAYABR}"."?|{DAYFUL})|{MON}{W}{INT}\
(st|nd|rd|th)){W})?{TIMEMOD}{EW}        |
{INT}"/"{INT}"/"{INT}                   |
{INT}"-"{MON}"-"{INT}                   |
the{W}{ORD19}({W}day)?{W}of{W}{MON}{EW} |
(today|tonight|tomorrow|yesterday)      { ADDDATE; havedate++; }

(of|in){W}{YEAR}                        |
```

```
","{W}{YEAR}                    { if (havedate)
                                 { register char *s=yytext+yyleng-4;
                                   if (*s == 'l') *s = '1';
                                   ADDDATE;
                                   havedate++;
                                 }
                                 else
                                 { char tmp[64];
                                   strcpy (tmp, yytext);
                                   tmp[yyleng-4] = '\0';
                                   dotext (tmp);
                                   setnum (atof (yytext+yyleng-4));
                                 }
                               }

today[']s{W}date{W}in{W}{YEAR}  |
this{W}(date|day){W}in{W}{YEAR} |
today{W}in{W}{YEAR}            { register char *s = yytext+yyleng-4;
                                if (*s == 'l') *s = '1';
                                realyear = atoi (s);
                                strcat (datestr, "today");
                                havedate++; }

(({INT}|{CARD19}|the){W}days?{W}(before|after)) { ADDDATE; }
(at({W}about)?|around|on({W}or{W}(around|about))?) {
                                if (havedate)
                                { strcat (datestr," at "); }
                                else
                                { dotext (yytext); }
                               }

{ID}                           { FLUSH dotext (yytext); }

/* Mark paragraph and sentence boundaries */

[.!?]([ \t]*\n)([ \t]*\n)+     { FLUSH tbuf[0] = yytext[0];
                                tbuf[1] = '\0';
                                text (tbuf);
                                if (!inspec)
                                  marker ('p', yyftell());
                               }

[.!?](\n|" "|\t)[ \t]*         { FLUSH tbuf[0] = yytext[0];
                                tbuf[1] = '\0';
                                text (tbuf);
                                if (!inspec)
                                  marker ('s', yyftell());
                               }

^([ \t]*\n)+                   { FLUSH
                                if (!inspec)
                                  marker ('p', yyftell());
                               }
\n                             { if (havedate)           ADDDATE;
```

```
                                else if (innumber ()) eatnl ();
                                else ; /* Ignore it in text */
                        }
                        { FLUSH dotext (yytext); }

%%

/***********************************************************************
 * number routines
 ***********************************************************************/

double r1 = 0.0, r2 = 0.0, lastmult=0.0, scale=0.0, atof();
int h1=0, h2=0, digit=0, isord=0, atenl=0, atoi();

innumber ()
{ return (h1 || h2); }

setnum (x)
double x;
{ if (innumber ()) flushnum ();
  r1 = x; h1++;
}

eatnl ()
{ atenl++; }

addtrip (n)
int n;
{ r1 = r1 * 1000.0 + n; h1++; }

double getnum ()
{ double result = 0.0;

  endmult ();
  if (h1) { r2 += r1; h1=0; h2++; }
  if (h2)
  { result = r2; }
  r1 = r2 = 0.0; h1 = h2 = digit = 0;
  return (result);
}

flushnum ()
{
  if (innumber ())
  { char buf[BUFSIZ];
    double result = getnum ();

    if (result == 1.0)
    { text (isord ? "first" : "one"); }

    else if (result == 2.0 && isord)
    { text ("second"); }

    else
```

```
    { sprintf (buf, "(%s %lg)",
                 isord ? "ordinal" : "number", result);
      settext (); printonetoken (first ? "" : " ", buf);
      first = 0;
    }
  }

  r1 = r2 = 0.0; h1 = h2 = digit = isord = atenl = 0;
}

special (text)
char *text;
{
  settext (); printonetoken (" ", text);
}

ordinal ()
{ isord++;
  flushnum ();
}

adddigit (n)
int n;
{ if (lastmult == 100.0)
  { endmult (); r1 += n; h1++; }
  else
  { endmult ();
    if (digit)  { r1 += n; h1++; digit = 0; }
    else        { r1 = r1 * 10.0 + n; h1++; }
  }
}

addteen (n)
int n;
{ if (lastmult == 100.0)
  { endmult (); r1 += n; h1++; }
  else
  { endmult (); r1 = r1 * 100.0 + n; h1++; }
}

addenty (n)
{ if (lastmult == 100.0)
  { endmult (); r1 += n; h1++; digit++; }
  else
  { endmult (); r1 = r1 * 100.0 + n; h1++; digit++; }
}

endmult ()
{ if (scale != 0.0)
  { r1 *= scale;
    if (r1 > 1000.0)
    { r2 += r1; r1 = 0.0; h2++; h1 = 0; }
  }
  lastmult = scale = 0.0;
```

```
}

addmult (x)
double x;
{ if (lastmult == 0 || scale == 0)
  { scale = x; lastmult = x; }
  else if (x > lastmult)
  { scale *= x; lastmult = x; }
  else
  { endmult (); r1 = x; h1++; lastmult = x; scale = 1.0; }
}

addfrac (x)
double x;
{ r1 += x; h1++; }

dofraction (num, den)
double num, den;
{ char buf[BUFSIZ];

  sprintf (buf, "(fraction %lg %lg)%s", num, den, atenl ? "\n" : " ");
  settext ();
  printonetoken (" ", buf);

  r1 = r2 = 0.0; h1 = h2 = digit = isord = atenl = 0;
}

orddigit (n, plural)
int n;
int plural;
{
  if (plural || r1 == 1.0 && h2 == 0.0)
  { dofraction (getnum (), (double) n); }
  else
  { adddigit (n);
    ordinal ();
  }
}

ordteen (n, plural)
int n;
int plural;
{
  if (plural || r1 == 1.0 && h2 == 0.0)
  { dofraction (getnum (), (double) n); }
  else
  { addteen (n);
    ordinal ();
  }
}

ordenty (n, plural)
int n;
int plural;
```

```
{
  if (plural || r1 == 1.0 && h2 == 0.0)
  { dofraction (getnum (), (double) n); }
  else
  { addenty (n);
    ordinal ();
  }
}

ordmult (x, plural)
double x;
int plural;
{
  if (plural || r1 == 1.0 && h2 == 0.0)
  { dofraction (getnum (), x); }
  else
  { addmult (x);
    ordinal ();
  }
}
```

REFERENCES

[AI Journal 90]
AI Journal, *Special Issue on Machine Learning*, AI, Vol. 40, 1990.

[Alshawi 87]
H. Alshawi, "Processing Dictionary Definitions with Phrasal Pattern Hierarchies," *Computational Linguistics*, Vol. 13, No. 3-4, July-December 1987, pp. 195-202.

[Amsler 80]
R. A. Amsler, *The Structure of the Merriam-Webster Pocket Dictionary*, PhD dissertation, The University of Texas at Austin, December 1980.

[Amsler 81]
R. A. Amsler, "A Taxonomy for English Nouns and Verbs," *Proceedings of the 19th Annual Meeting of the Association for Computational Linguistics*, June 1981, pp. 133-138.

[Arms & Holzhauser 88]
W. Y. Arms and L. D. Holzhauser, "MERCURY: An Electronic Library", Carnegie Mellon University and The Online Computer Library Center internal report.

[Belew 87a]
R. Belew, *Adaptive Information Retrieval: Machine Learning in Associative Networks*, PhD dissertation, University of Michigan, January 1987.

[Belew 87b]
R. Belew, 1987. Private communication.

[Bell Labs 79]
D. Ritchie and K. Thompson, "The Unix Programmer's Manual," Tech. report, Bell Telephone Laboratories, 1979.

[Bentley 85]
J. Bentley, "A Spelling Checker," *Comm. ACM*, Vol. 28, No. 5, May 1985, pp. 456-462.

[Berwick 84]
R. C. Berwick, "Bounded Context Parsing and Easy Learnability," *Proceedings of the Tenth International Conference on Computational Linguistics*, July 1984, pp. 20-23.

[Bethke 81]
A. D. Bethke, *Genetic Algorithms as Function Optimizers*, PhD dissertation, University of Michigan, January 1981.

[Binot & Jensen 87]
J.-L. Binot and K. Jensen, "A Semantic Expert Using an Online Standard Dictionary," *Proceedings of the Tenth International Joint Conference on Artificial Intelligence*, August 1987, pp. 709-714.

[Blair & Maron 85a]
D. C. Blair and M. E. Maron, "An Evaluation of Retrieval Effectiveness for a Full-Text Document-Retrieval System," *Comm. ACM*, Vol. 28, No. 3, March 1985, pp. 289-299.

[Blair & Maron 85b]
D. C. Blair and M. E. Maron, "Author's Response," *Comm. ACM*, Vol. 28, No. 11, November 1985, pp. 1240-1242.

[Bobrow & Winograd 77]
D. G. Bobrow and T. Winograd, "An Overview of KRL, a Knowledge Representation Language," *Cognitive Science*, Vol. 1, No. 1, 1977, pp. 3-46.

[Boguraev & Briscoe 87]
B. Boguraev and T. Briscoe, "Large Lexicons for Natural Language Processing: Utilizing the Grammar Coding System of LDOCE," *Computational Linguistics*, Vol. 13, No. 3-4, July-December 1987, pp. 203-219.

[Borenstein et al. 88]
N. S. Borenstein, C. F. Everhardt, J. Rosenberg, and A. Stoller, "A Multi-media Message System for Andrew," *Proceedings of the USENIX Association Winter Conference*, February 1988, pp. 37-42.

[Brachman 79]
R. J. Brachman, "On the epistemological status of semantic networks," in *Associative Networks: Representation and Use of Knowledge by Computers*, N. V. Findler, ed., Academic Press, New York, 1979, pp. 3-50, Also in [Brachman & Levesque 85].

[Brachman & Levesque 85]
R. J. Brachman and H. J. Levesque, *Readings in Knowledge Representation*, Morgan Kaufman, Los Altos, CA, 1985.

[Bradley 86]
E. Bradley, "Sixty Minutes", CBS News, March 23, 1986.

[Brand 87]
S. Brand, *The Media Lab: Inventing the future at M.I.T.*, Viking Press, New York, 1987.

[Brzustowicz 80]

M. A. Brzustowicz, "A System for the Implementation of Models of Reasoning with Uncertain Data," Master's thesis, Carnegie-Mellon University, Computer Science Department, July1980.

[Burnham 83]

David Burnham, *The Rise of the Computer State*, Random House, Inc., New York, 1983.

[Cameron 72]

J. S. Cameron, *Automatic Document Pseudoclassification and Retrieval by Word Frequency Techniques*, PhD dissertation, Ohio State University, 1972.

[Carbonell 79]

J. G. Carbonell, "Towards a Self-Extending Parser," *Proceedings of the 17th Annual Meeting of the Association for Computational Linguistics*, August 1979, pp. 3-7.

[Carbonell 80]

J. G. Carbonell, "Default Reasoning and Inheritance Mechanisms on Type Hierarchies," *SIGART, SIGPLAN, SIGMOD Joint volume on Data Abstraction*, 1980.

[Carbonell 81]

J. G. Carbonell, "Towards a Robust, Task-Oriented Natural Language Interface," *Workshop/Symposium on Human Computer Interaction*, A. N. Badler,ed., Georgia Tech Information Sciences, March 1981.

[Carbonell 82]

J. G. Carbonell, "Metaphor: An Inescapable Phenomenon in Natural Language Comprehension," in *Strategies for Natural Language Processing*, W. Lehnert and M. Ringle, eds., Erlbaum, New Jersey, 1982, pp. 415-434.

[Carbonell & Brzustowicz 84]

J. G. Carbonell and M. A. Brzustowicz, "Partial Pattern Matching and Evidentiary Combination," Tech. report, Carnegie-Mellon University, Computer Science Department, 1984.

[Carbonell & Hayes 81]

J. G. Carbonell and P. J. Hayes, "Dynamic Strategy Selection in Flexible Parsing," *Proceedings of the 19th Annual Meeting of the Association for Computational Linguistics*, 1981.

[Carbonell & Joseph 85]

J. G. Carbonell and R. Joseph, "The FRAMEKIT+ Reference Manual", CMU Computer Science Department internal paper.

[Carbonell & Thomason 86]
    J. G. Carbonell and R. H. Thomason, "Parsing in Biomedical Indexing and Retrieval," *AAMSI-86*, 1986.

[Carbonell et al. 83a]
    J. G. Carbonell, W. M. Boggs, M. L. Mauldin and P. G. Anick, "The XCALIBUR Project, A Natural Language Interface to Expert Systems," *Proceedings of the Eighth International Joint Conference on Artificial Intelligence*, 1983.

[Carbonell et al. 83b]
    J. G. Carbonell, W. M. Boggs, M. L. Mauldin and P. G. Anick, "XCALIBUR Project Report 1: First Steps Towards an Integrated Natural Language Interface," Tech. report CMU-CS-83-143, Carnegie-Mellon University, Computer Science Department, July 1983.

[Carbonell et al. 84]
    J. G. Carbonell, D. A. Evans and D. S. Scott, "Toward the Automation of Content-Access Methods for Large-scale Textual Databases", Technical Proposal RFP No. NLM-84-115/PSP, Carnegie-Mellon University, Computer Science Department, 1984.

[Carbonell et al. 85a]
    J. G. Carbonell, D. A. Evans, D. S. Scott and R. H. Thomason, "Final Report on the Automated Classification and Retrieval Project," Tech. report, Carnegie Mellon University, Departments of Philosophy and Computer Science, December 1985.

[Carbonell et al. 85b]
    J. G. Carbonell, W. M. Boggs, M. L. Mauldin and P. G. Anick, "The XCALIBUR Project, A Natural Language Interface to Expert Systems and Data Bases," in *Applications in Artificial Intelligence*, S. Andriole, ed., Petrocelli Books Inc., 1985.

[Carnegie Group 89]
    Carnegie Group, Inc., "Text Categorization Shell," Technical Brief, CGI, August 1989.

[Chiaramella & Defude 87]
    Y. Chiaramella and B. Defude, "A Prototype of an Intelligent System for Information Retrieval: Iota," *Information Processing and Management*, Vol. 23, No. 4, 1987, pp. 285-303.

[Clarke 79]
    A. C. Clarke, *The Fountains of Paradise*, Harcourt Brace Jovanovich, New York, 1979.

[Croft 87]
    W. B. Croft, "Approaches to Intelligent Information Retrieval," *Information Processing and Management*, Vol. 23, No. 4, 1987, pp. 249-254.

[Cursor 86]
J. Gray, "The Computer and the Big Dictionary," *Cursor: The Computing Newsletter of Carnegie-Mellon*, Vol. 3, No. 4, April 1986, pp. 3-5, Reprinted from the University of Waterloo's *Computing Services Newsletter*, Issue 1985-01, which was adapted from Princeton's *Virtual News*, Vol. 6, No. 5, Jan. 1986, pp. 6-7, 11.

[Deerwester et al. 90]
S. Deerwester, S. T. Dumais, G. W. Furnas, T. K. Landauer and R. Harshman, "Indexing by Latent Semantic Analysis," *JASIS*, Vol. 41, No. 6, September 1990, pp. 391-407.

[DeJong, G. 79a]
G. F. DeJong, *Skimming Stories in Real Time: An Experiment in Integrated Understanding*, PhD dissertation, Yale University, 1979.

[DeJong, G. 79b]
G. F. DeJong, "Prediction and Substantiation: a New Approach to Natural Language Processing," *Cognitive Science*, Vol. 3, September 1979.

[Dejong, G. 81]
G. F. DeJong, "Automatic Schema Acquisition in a Natural Language Environment," *Proceedings of the 19th Annual Meeting of the Association for Computational Linguistics*, The Association for Computational Linguistics, 1981, pp. 410-413.

[DeJong, G. 82]
G. F. DeJong, "An Overview of the FRUMP System," in *Strategies for Natural Language Processing*, W. G. Lehnert and M. H. Ringle, ed., Lawrence Erlbaum Associates, Hillsdale, NJ, 1982, pp. 149-176, ch. 5.

[DeJong, G. 83a]
G. F. DeJong, "An Approach to Learning from Observation," *Proceedings of the Second International Machine Learning Conference*, July 1983.

[DeJong, G. 83b]
G. F. DeJong, "Acquiring Schemata Through Understanding and Generalizing Plans," *Proceedings of the Eighth International Joint Conference on Artificial Intelligence*, August 1983, pp. 463-464.

[DeJong, K. 75]
K. A. DeJong, *Analysis of the Behavior of a Class of Genetic Adaptive Systems*, PhD dissertation, University of Michigan, August 1975.

[DeJong, K. 80]
K. A. DeJong, "Adaptive System Design: A Genetic Approach," *IEEE Transactions on Man, Systems and Cybernetics*, Vol. 10, No. 9, September 1980.

[DeJong, K. & Smith, T. 81]
    K. A. DeJong and T. Smith, "Genetic Algorithms Applied to Infor-
    mation Driven Models of US Migration Patterns," *12th Annual Pitts-
    burgh Conference on Modeling and Simulation*, April 1981.

[Dumais 90]
    S. T. Dumais, "Enhancing Performance in Latent Semantic Indexing
    (LSI) Retrieval", In preparation.

[Dumais et al. 88]
    S. T. Dumais, G. W. Furnas and T. K. Landauer, "Using Latent
    Semantic Analysis to Improve Access to Textual Information,"
    Proceedings of the Computer Human Interaction Conference, 1988, pp.
    281-285.

[Evans et al. 91]
    D. A. Evans, K. Ginther-Webster, M. Hart, R. G. Lefferts and
    I. A. Monarch, "Automatic Indexing Using Selective NLP and First-
    Order Thesauri," *RIAO 91 Conference Proceedings: Intelligent Text
    and Image Handling*, April 1991, pp. 624-643.

[Fagan 87a]
    J. L. Fagan, "Automatic Phrase Indexing for Document Retrieval: An
    Examination of Syntactic and Non-syntactic Methods," *Proceedings of
    the Tenth Annual International ACMSIGIR Conference on Research
    and Development in Information Retrieval*, Association for Computing
    Machinery, New York, 1987, pp. 91-101.

[Fagan 87b]
    J. L. Fagan, *Experiments in Automatic Phrase Indexing For Document
    Retrieval: A Comparison of Syntactic and Non-Syntactic Methods*, PhD
    dissertation, Cornell, September 1987.

[Fain et al. 85]
    J. Fain, J. G. Carbonell, P. J. Hayes and S. N. Minton, "MULTIPAR: a
    Robust Entity-Oriented Parser," *Proceedings of the Seventh Cognitive
    Science Society Conference*, Irvine, CA, 1985, pp. 110-119.

[Fillmore 68]
    C. J. Fillmore, "The Case for Case," in *The Universals of Linguistic
    Theory*, E. Bach and R. T. Harms, eds., Holt, Rinehart and Winston,
    New York, 1968, pp. 1-88.

[Flass 85]
    P. R. Flass, "Technical Correspondence," *Comm. ACM*, Vol. 28, No.
    11, November 1985, pp. 1238.

[Fogel et al. 66]
    L. J. Fogel, A. J. Owens and M. J. Walsh, *Artificial Intelligence
    Through Simulated Evolution*, Wiley, New York, 1966.

[Forrest 85]
S. Forrest, "Implementing Semantic Network Structures Using the Classifier System," *Proceedings of an International Conference on Genetic Algorithms and Their Applications*, J. J. Greffenstette,ed., July 1985, pp. 24-44.

[Fox 87]
E. A. Fox, "Development of the CODER System: A Testbed for Artificial Intelligence Methods in Information Retrieval," *Information Processing and Management*, Vol. 23, No. 4, 1987, pp. 341-366.

[Furnas et al. 88]
G. W. Furnas, S. Deerwester, S. T. Dumais, T. K. Landauer, R. A. Harshman, L. A. Streeter and K. E. Lochbaum, "Information Retrieval using a Singular Value Decomposition Model of Latent Semantic Structure," *SIGIR88*, ACM Press, June 1988, pp. 465-480, (SIGIR-88)

[Garey & Johnson 79]
M. R. Garey and D. S. Johnson, *Computers and Intractability: a Guide to the theory of NP-Completeness*, W. H. Freeman, San Francisco, 1979.

[Gosling 83]
J. Gosling, "Unix Emacs," Tech. report, Carnegie-Mellon University, Computer Science Department, 1983.

[Granger 77]
R. H. Granger, "FOULUP: A Program That Figures Out Meanings of Words from Context," *Proceedings of the Fifth International Joint Conference on Artificial Intelligence*, August 1977, pp. 172-178.

[Granger 82]
R. H. Granger, "Scruffy Text Understanding: Design and Implementation of 'Tolerant' Understanders," *Proceedings of the 20th Annual Meeting of the Association for Computational Linguistics*, June 1982, pp. 157-160.

[Green et al. 63]
B. F. Green, A. K. Wolf, C. Chomsky and K. Laughery, "Baseball: An Automatic Question Answerer," in *Computer and Thought*, E. A. Feigenbaum and J. Feldman, eds., McGraw-Hill, 1963, pp. 207-216.

[Greffenstette 84]
J. J. Greffenstette, "Optimization of Genetic Search Algorithms," Tech. report, Vanderbilt University, Computer Science Department, 1984.

[Grishman & Hirschman 78]
R. Grishman and L. Hirschman, "Question Answering from Natural Language Medical Databases," *AI*, Vol. 11, 1978, pp. 25-43.

[Grolier 85]
  "Academic American Encyclopedia", 1985.

[Haskin 80]
  R. L. Haskin, *Hardware for Searching Very Large Text Databases*, PhD dissertation, University of Illinois at Urbana-Champaign, 1980.

[Haskin 83]
  R. L. Haskin, "Operational Characteristics of a Hardware-Based Pattern Matcher," *ACM Transactions on Database Systems*, Vol. 8, No. 1, March 1983, pp. 15-40.

[Hayes, Knecht and Cellio 87]
  P. J. Hayes, L. E. Knecht and M. J. Cellio, "A News Story Categorization System," *Applied ACL Conference*, The Association for Computational Linguistics, 1987.

[Hendrix & Walter 87]
  G. G. Hendrix and B. A. Walter, "The Intelligent Assistant: Technical considerations involved in designing Q&A's natural language interface," *Byte*, December 1987, pp. 251-258.

[Hendrix et al. 76]
  G. G. Hendrix, E. D. Sacerdoti and J. Slocum, "Developing a Natural Language Interface to Complex Data," Tech. report Artificial Intelligence Center, SRI International, 1976.

[Holland 75]
  J. H. Holland, *Adaptation in Natural and Artificial Systems*, The University of Michigan Press, 1975.

[Holland 80]
  J. H. Holland, "Adaptive Algorithms for Discovery and Using General Patterns in Growing Knowledge Bases," *Intl. Journal of Policy Analysis and Info. Systems*, Vol. 4, No. 2, 1980.

[Holland 83]
  J. H. Holland, "Escaping Brittleness," *Proceedings of the Second International Machine Learning Conference*, July 1983.

[Horton 83]
  M. Horton, "How to Read the Network News," Tech. report, AT&T Bell Laboratories, 1983.

[Jacobson 89]
  G. J. Jacobson, *Succinct Data Structures*, PhD dissertation, Carnegie Mellon University, 1989.

[Jensen 86]
  K. Jensen, "PEG 1986: A Broad-Coverage Computational Syntax of English," Tech. report, IBM Thomas J. Watson Research Center, 1986.

[Jensen & Binot 87]
   K. Jensen and J.-L. Binot, "Disambiguating Prepositional Phrase Attachments by Using On-Line Dictionary Definitions," *Computational Linguistics*, Vol. 13, No. 3-4, July-December 1987, pp. 251-260.

[Katke 85a]
   W. Katke, "Learning Language Using a Pattern Recognition Approach," *AI Magazine*, Vol. 6, No. 1, Spring 1985, pp. 64-73.

[Katke 85b]
   W. Katke, personal communication, 1985.

[King 81]
   J. J. King, *Query Optimization by Semantic Reasoning*, PhD dissertation, Stanford University, 1981.

[Landauer & Littman 90]
   T. K. Landauer and M. L. Littman, "Fully Automatic Cross-Language Document Retrieval Using Latent Semantic Indexing", In preparation.

[Langley 82]
   P. Langley, "A Model of Early Syntactic Development," *Proceedings of the 20th Annual Meeting of the Association for Computational Linguistics*, June 1982, pp. 145-151.

[Langley et al. 83]
   P. Langley, J. Zytkow, H. A. Simon and G. L. Bradshaw, "Mechanisms for Qualitative and Quantitative Discovery," *Proceedings of the Second International Machine Learning Conference*, July 1983.

[Lebowitz 85a]
   M. Lebowitz, "RESEARCHER: An Experimental Intelligent Information System," *Proceedings of the Eighth International Joint Conference on Artificial Intelligence*, August 1985, pp. 858-862.

[Lebowitz 85b]
   M. Lebowitz, "An Experiment in Intelligent Information Systems: RESEARCHER," Tech. report, Columbia University, Dept. of Computer Science, Nov 1985.

[Lebowitz 85c]
   M. Lebowitz, "The Use of Memory in Text Processing," Tech. report, Columbia University, Dept. of Computer Science, Nov 1985.

[Lebowitz 86]
   M. Lebowitz, "Integrated Learning: Controlling Explanation," *Cognitive Science*, Vol. 10, No. 2, April-June 1986, pp. 219-240.

[Lehman 89]
   J. F. Lehman, *Adaptive Parsing: Self-extending Natural Language Interfaces*, PhD dissertation, Carnegie Mellon University, August 1989.

[Lehman & Carbonell 88]
J. F. Lehman and J. G. Carbonell, "Learning the User's Language, a Step Towards Automated Creation of User Models," in *User Modelling in Dialog Systems*, W. Wahlster and A. Kobsa, eds., Springer-Verlag, 1988.

[Lenat 79]
D. B. Lenat, "Automated Theory Formation in Mathematics," *Proceedings of the Sixth International Joint Conference on Artificial Intelligence*, 1979.

[Lenat & Brown 83]
D. B. Lenat and J. S. Brown, "Why AM and Eurisko Appear to Work," *Proceedings of the National Conference on Artificial Intelligence*, August 1983.

[Lenat & Guha 88]
D. B. Lenat and R. V. Guha, "The World According to CYC," Tech. report ACA-AI-300-88, M.C.C., September 1988.

[Lenat et al. 83]
D. B. Lenat, F. Hayes-Roth and P. Klahr, "Cognitive Economy," *Proceedings of the Second International Machine Learning Conference*, July 1983.

[Lesk 85]
M. E. Lesk, "SIGIR 85," *ACM SIGIR Forum*, Vol. 18, No. 2-4, Fall 1985, pp. 10-15.

[Lesk & Schmidt 75]
M. E. Lesk and E. Schmidt, "Lex — A Lexical Analyzer Generator," Tech. report, Bell Laboratories, 1975.

[Lewis, D. A. E. 84]
D. A. E. Lewis, *Case Grammar and Functional Relations in Aboutness Recognition and Relevance Decision-Making in the Bibliographic Retrieval Environment*, PhD dissertation, University of Western Ontario, July 1984, National Library of Canada index TC-61778. As cited in [Lewis, D. D. 87].

[Lewis, D. D. 87]
D. D. Lewis, 1987. Private communication, a review of Dee Ann Emmel Lewis's PhD Thesis [Lewis, D. A. E. 84].

[Lewis, D. D., Croft & Bhandaru 89]
D. D. Lewis, W. B. Croft and N. Bhandaru, "Language-Oriented Information Retrieval," *International Journal of Intelligent Systems*, Vol. 4, No. 3, Fall 1989.

[Lindsay 63]

R. K. Lindsay, "Inferential Memory as the Basis of Machines Which Understand Natural Language," in *Computer and Thought*, E. A. Feigenbaum and J. Feldman, eds., McGraw-Hill, 1963, pp. 217-233.

[Maarek 87]

Y. S. Maarek, "On the Use of Cluster Analysis for Assisting Maintenance of Large Software Systems", Thesis Proposal, Computer Science Department, Technion, Israel Institute of Technology, Haifa.

[Malone et al. 87]

T. W. Malone, K. R. Grant, F. A. Turbak, S. A. Brobst, and M. D. Cohen, "Intelligent Information-Sharing Systems," *Comm. ACM*, Vol. 30, No. 5, May 1987, pp. 390-402.

[Mathis 72]

B. A. Mathis, *Techniques for the Evaluation and Improvement of Computer-Produced Abstracts*, PhD dissertation, Ohio State University, 1972.

[Mauldin 84a]

M. L. Mauldin, "Semantic Rule Based Text Generation," *Proceedings of the Tenth International Conference on Computational Linguistics*, July 1984.

[Mauldin 84b]

M. L. Mauldin, "Maintaining Diversity in Genetic Search," *Proceedings of the National Conference on Artificial Intelligence*, August 1984.

[Mauldin 86a]

M. L. Mauldin, "Retrieving Information with a Text Skimming Parser," *Proceedings of the 1986 Eastern States Conference on Linguistics*, October 1986.

[Mauldin 86b]

M. L. Mauldin, "Information Retrieval by Text Skimming", Carnegie-Mellon University, Computer Science Department

[Mauldin et al. 87]

M. L. Mauldin, J. G. Carbonell and R. H. Thomason, "Beyond the Keyword Barrier: Knowledge-Based Information Retrieval," *Information Services and Use*, Vol. 7, March 1987, Paper presented at the 29th Annual Conference of the National Federation of Abstracting and Information Services.

[McCune et al. 85]

B. P. McCune, R. M. Tong, J. S. Dean and D. G. Shapiro, "RUBRIC: A System for Rule-based Information Retrieval," *IEEE Transactions on Software Engineering*, Vol. SE-11, No. 9, September 1985, pp. 939-945.

[McMaster 75]
I. McMaster, "A Proposal for Computer Acquisition of Natural Language," Tech. report TR-75-3, Dept. of Computer Science, University of Alberta, May 1975.

[Merriam 74]
G. & C. Merriam Co., *The Merriam-Webster Dictionary*, Simon and Schuster, New York, 1974.

[Metzler et al. 84]
D. P. Metzler, T. Noreault, L. Richey and B. Heidorn, "Dependency Parsing for Information Retrieval," *Research and Development in Information Retrieval*, C. J. van Rijsbergen,ed., Cambridge University Press, July 1984, pp. 313-324.

[Michalski et al. 83]
R. S. Michalski, J. G. Carbonell and T. M. Mitchell (Eds.), *Machine Learning, An Artificial Intelligence Approach*, Tioga Press, 1983.

[Minsky 75]
M. Minsky, "A Framework for Representing Knowledge," in *The Psychology of Computer Vision*, P. Winston, ed., McGraw-Hill, New York, 1975.

[Mitchell 77]
T. M. Mitchell, "Version Spaces: A Candidate Elimination Approach to Rule Learning," *Proceedings of the Fifth International Joint Conference on Artificial Intelligence*, August 1977, pp. 305-310.

[Monarch & Carbonell 86]
I. Monarch and J. G. Carbonell, "Final Report on COALSORT: A Knowledge-Based Interface to an Information Retrieval System," Tech. report, Carnegie Mellon University, Department of Computer Science, 1986.

[Mooney & DeJong 85]
R. Mooney and G. F. DeJong, "Learning Schemata for Natural Language Processing," *Proceedings of the Ninth International Joint Conference on Artificial Intelligence*, August 1985, pp. 681-687.

[Nyberg 88]
E. Nyberg, "The FrameKit User's Guide," Technical Memo, Center for Machine Translation, Carnegie Mellon University, 1988.

[Obermeier 87]
K. K. Obermeier, "Natural Language Processing: An introductory look at some of the technology used in this area of artificial intelligence," *Byte*, December 1987, pp. 225-233.

[Oddy 81]
R. N. Oddy et al., *Information Retrieval Research*, Butterworths, London, 1981.

[Orgren 79]
P. J. Orgren, *The Induction of the Syntax of Natural Language by Computer*, PhD dissertation, University of Wisconsin — Madison, 1979.

[Peterson 82]
J. L. Peterson, "Webster's Seventh New Collegiate Dictionary: A Computer-Readable File Format," Tech. report TR-196, Dept. of Computer Sciences, University of Texas at Austin, May 1982.

[Quirk et al. 72]
R. Quirk, S. Greenbaum, G. Leech and J. Svartvik, *A Grammar of Contemporary English*, Longman, London, 1972.

[Raphael 68]
B. Raphael, "SIR: Semantic Information Retrieval," in *Semantic Information Processing*, M. Minksy, ed., MIT Press, Cambridge, Mass., 1968, pp. 33-145, ch. 2.

[Rau 87]
L. F. Rau, "Knowledge Organization and Access in a Conceptual Information System," *Information Processing and Management*, Vol. 23, No. 4, 1987, pp. 269-283.

[Rendell 83]
L. A. Rendell, "A Doubly Layered, Genetic Penetrance Learning System," *Proceedings of the National Conference on Artificial Intelligence*, August 1983, pp. 343-347.

[Rich 79]
E. Rich, *Building and Exploiting User Models*, PhD dissertation, Carnegie Mellon University, April 1979.

[Rich 83]
E. Rich, *Artificial Intelligence*, McGraw-Hill, New York, McGraw-Hill Series in Artificial Intelligence, 1983.

[Riesbeck 82]
C. K. Riesbeck, "Realistic Language Comprehension," in *Strategies for Natural Language Processing*, W. G. Lehnert and M. H. Ringle, ed., Lawrence Erlbaum Associates, Hillsdale, NJ, 1982, pp. 37-54, ch. 2.

[Sager 81]
N. Sager, *Natural Language Information Processing, A Computer Grammar of English and Its Applications*, Addison-Wesley, Reading, Mass., 1981.

[Salton 73]
G. Salton, "Recent Studies in Automatic Text Analysis and Document Retrieval," *J. ACM*, Vol. 20, No. 2, April 1973, pp. 258-278.

[Salton 86]
G. Salton, "Another Look at Automatic Text-Retrieval Systems," *Comm. ACM*, Vol. 29, No. 7, July 1986, pp. 648-656.

[Salton & Lesk 68]
G. Salton and M. E. Lesk, "Computer Evaluation of Indexing and Text Processing," *J. ACM*, Vol. 15, No. 1, January 1968, pp. 8-36.

[Salton & McGill 83]
G. Salton and M. J. McGill, *Introduction to Modern Information Retrieval*, McGraw-Hill, New York, McGraw-Hill Computer Science Series, 1983.

[Schank & Riesbeck 81]
R. C. Schank and C. K. Riesbeck, *Inside Computer Understanding*, Lawrence Erlbaum Associates, Hillsdale, NJ, 1981.

[Schank et al. 75]
R. C. Schank, N. M. Goldman, C. J. Rieger and C. K. Riesbeck, *Conceptual Information Processing*, North-Holland, Amsterdam, Fundamental Studies in Computer Science, Vol. 3, 1975.

[Schildt 87]
H. Schildt, "Natural Language Processing in C," *Byte*, December 1987, pp. 269-276.

[Seaman 86]
P. Seaman, "Technical Correspondence," *Comm. ACM*, Vol. 29, No. 2, February 1986, pp. 148-149.

[Shaw 80]
D. E. Shaw, *Knowledge-based Retrieval on a Relational Database Machine*, PhD dissertation, Stanford University, 1980.

[Simmons 87]
R. F. Simmons, "A Text Knowledge Base from the AI Handbook," *Information Processing and Management*, Vol. 23, No. 4, 1987, pp. 321-339.

[Smith, B. 89]
B. Smith, "The Unix Connection," *BYTE Magazine*, Vol. 14, No. 5, May 1989, pp. 245-251.

[Smith, P. 87]
P. J. Smith, "Bibliographic Information Retrieval Systems: increasing cognitive compatibility," *Information Services and Use*, Vol. 7, March 1987, Paper presented at the 29th Annual Conference of the National Federation of Abstracting and Information Services.

[Smith, S. 80]
S. F. Smith, *A Learning System Based on Genetic Adaptive Algorithms,* PhD dissertation, University of Pittsburgh, 1980.

[Smith, S. 83]
S. F. Smith, "Flexible Learning of Problem Solving Heuristics through Adaptive Search," *Proceedings of the Eighth International Joint Conference on Artificial Intelligence,* August 1983, pp. 422-425.

[Smith, S. 84]
S. F. Smith, "Adaptive Learning Systems," in *Expert Systems — Principles and Case Studies,* R. Forsyth, ed., Associated Book Publishers, Ltd., 1984.

[Sparck Jones 91]
K. Sparck Jones, "Notes and References on Early Classification Work," *ACM SIGIR Forum,* Vol. 25, No. 1, Spring 1991, pp. 10-17.

[Sparck Jones & Tait 84]
K. Sparck Jones and J. I. Tait, "Linguistically Motivated Descriptive Term Selection," *Proceedings of the Tenth International Conference on Computational Linguistics,* COLING, July 1984, pp. 287-290.

[Sparck Jones & Wilks 83]
K. Sparck Jones and Y. Wilks, *Automatic Natural Language Parsing,* Halsted Press, Chichester, 1983.

[Stepp 84]
R. E. Stepp, *Conjunctive Conceptual Clustering,* PhD dissertation, University of Illinois at Urbana-Champaign, 1984.

[Teskey 82]
F. N. Teskey, *Principles of Text Processing,* John Wiley & Sons, New York, 1982.

[Time 86]
P. Elmer-DeWitt, "An Electronic Assault on Privacy?," *Time,* May 19 1986, pp. 104.

[Tomita 86]
M. Tomita, *Efficient Parsing for Natural Language,* Kluwer Academic Pulishers, 1986.

[Tong et al. 86]
R. M. Tong, L. A. Appelbaum, V. N. Askman and J. F. Cunningham, "RUBRIC III: An Object-Oriented Expert System for Information Retrieval," *Second Annual Conference on Expert Systems In Government,* McLean, VA, October 1986.

[Touretzky 86]
D. S. Touretzky, *The Mathematics of Inheritance Systems,* Morgan Kaufman, Los Altos, CA, 1986.

[Walker & Amsler 86]
D. E. Walker and R. A. Amsler, "The Use of Machine-Readable Dictionaries in Sublanguage Analysis," in *Analyzing Language Language in Restricted Domains*, R. Grishman and R. Kittredge, eds., Lawrence Erlbaum Associates, Hillsdale, NJ, 1986, pp. 69-83.

[Waltz 87]
D. L. Waltz, "Applications of the Connection Machine," *Computer*, Vol. 20, No. 1, January 1987, pp. 85 ff.

[Waterman 70]
D. A. Waterman, "Generalized Learning Techniques for Automating the Learning of Heuristics," *Artificial Intelligence*, Vol. 1, 1970.

[Waterman & Hayes-Roth 78]
D. A. Waterman and F. Hayes-Roth (Eds.), *Pattern-Directed Inference Systems*, Academic Press, 1978.

[Welch 84]
T. A. Welch, "A Technique for High Performance Data Compression," *IEEE Computer*, Vol. 17, No. 6, June 1984, pp. 8-19.

[Wessel 74]
A. E. Wessel, *Computer-aided Information Retrieval*, Melville Pub. Co., Los Angeles, 1974.

[Wexler & Culicover 80]
K. Wexler and P. Culicover, *Formal Principles of Language Acquisition*, MIT Press, Cambridge, MA, 1980, From reference section of [Berwick 84].

[Wilensky & Arens 80]
R. Wilensky and Y. Arens, "PHRAN: A Knowledge-Based Natural Language Understander," *Proceedings of the 18th Annual Meeting of the Association for Computational Linguistics*, June 1980, pp. 117-121.

[Winograd 83]
T. Winograd, *Language as a Cognitive Process*, Addison-Wesley, Reading, Mass., Vol. 1, 1983.

[Winston 84]
Winston, P. H., *Artificial Intelligence*, Addison-Wesley, Reading, Mass., 1984, Second Edition.

[Woods 75]
W. J. Woods, "What's in a Link: Foundations for Semantic Networks," in *Representation and Understanding: Issues in Cognitive Science*, D. G. Bobrow and A. M. Collins, eds., Academic Press, New York, 1975, pp. 35-82, Also in [Brachman & Levesque 85].

[Young, C. 73]
C. E. Young, *Development on Language Analysis Procedures with application to Automatic Indexing*, PhD dissertation, Ohio State University, 1973.

[Young, S. & Hayes 85]
S. R. Young and P. J. Hayes, "TESS: A Telex Classifying and Summarization System," *The Second Conference on Artificial Intelligence Applications*, IEEE, 1985.

[Young, S. and Haberlach 86]
S. R. Young and D. Haberlach, "A Natural Language Parser for Connected Text Processing", 1986. Unpublished.

[Yu 73]
C. T. Yu, *Theory of Indexing and Classification*, PhD dissertation, Cornell University, 1973.

[Zeidenberg 87]
M. Zeidenberg, "Modeling the Brain: A neural-network approach to natural language processing and similar problems may be the key to building systems that 'learn'," *Byte*, December 1987, pp. 237-246.

[Zernik & Dyer 87]
U. Zernik and M. G. Dyer, "The Self-Extending Phrasal Lexicon," *Computational Linguistics*, Vol. 13, No. 3-4, July-December 1987, pp. 308-327.

INDEX